queers.

Other Titles in this Series

queers.

eight monologues

curated by
Mark Gatiss

NICK HERN BOOKS
London
www.nickhernbooks.co.uk

A Nick Hern Book

Queers first published in Great Britain in 2017 as a paperback original by
Nick Hern Books Limited, The Glasshouse, 49a Goldhawk Road, London
W12 8QP, by arrangement with the BBC, and in association with the
BBC Studios production *Queers*

Introduction copyright © 2017 Mark Gatiss
The Man on the Platform © 2017 Mark Gatiss
The Perfect Gentleman © 2017 Jackie Clune
Safest Spot in Town © 2017 Keith Jarrett
Missing Alice © 2017 Jon Bradfield
I Miss the War © 2017 Matthew Baldwin
More Anger © 2017 Brian Fillis
A Grand Day Out © 2017 Michael Dennis
Something Borrowed © 2017 Gareth McLean

The authors have asserted their moral rights

Cover images (clockwise from top-left): Ben Whishaw, Gemma Whelan, Kadiff
Kirwan, Ian Gelder, Alan Cumming, Fionn Whitehead, Russell Tovey and
Rebecca Front in the BBC Studios production of *Queers*; copyright © BBC;
photographer: Richard Ansett

The 'BBC' wordmark and logo are trademarks of the British Broadcasting
Corporation and are used under licence. BBC Logo © BBC 1996

Designed and typeset by Nick Hern Books, London
Printed in Great Britain by CPI Books (UK) Ltd

A CIP catalogue record for this book is available from the British Library

ISBN   978 1 84842 696 2

MIX
Paper from
responsible sources
FSC
www.fsc.org   **FSC® C013604**

Contents

Introduction
Mark Gatiss

When I was a child, Friday nights were sacrosanct because it was then – after the late sports report – that Tyne Tees Television showed horror films. I would sometimes watch them in company, but more often than not I was left by myself to sit up and watch. In the summer, the slot was occupied by more palatable fare but, used to my horrors, my family duly left me alone. One night – I think I was about twelve or thirteen – there was a film called *If.* I knew nothing about it except the *Northern Echo* gave it five stars and a 'don't miss!'

An English public school. Boys returning from the holidays. And, within minutes, a beautiful blond boy is being castigated by a prefect with the words 'And you, Phillips, stop tarting.' I felt my heart thud in my chest, my mouth go dry. As the film unfolded, I found myself more tense and gripped than by any horror film I'd ever seen. I became more and more afraid that someone would come downstairs and catch me watching, spoil it all, spoil the illicit thrill…

I'd known I was gay since before I could really understand what such a thing meant. And, just as I had pored over the men's underwear section of the Brian Mills catalogue in search of titillation (it was slim pickings in those days), I had scoured the TV schedules for anything that might have even a glimmer of homosexual content. From my first crushes (Craig in *The Champions* and the dark one off *Follyfoot* in case you're wondering) to the first stirrings of something nameless and exciting whilst watching a particular adventure of *The Tomorrow People*. Jason Kemp, the actor in that episode later turned up in the ITV drama *Kids*, playing a brilliantly acerbic Scouse queen. I think I responded both to his physical beauty and his blazing queerness which, like all the best things, felt both exciting and a little bit scary.

These fragments, then, these little moments of visible gayness were like diamonds in the TV schedules. To be savoured, hoarded up and remembered forever.

These days, of course, we do not have to scour the schedules in the same way. There are visible gay characters in many mainstream dramas. Nevertheless, the commitment of the BBC to their 'Gay Britannia' season is still a massive cause for celebration. So when I was approached with the idea of curating a series of monologues for the fiftieth anniversary of the 1967 Sexual Offences Act, I leapt at the chance.

But where to start? Well, with a qualification. *Queers* commemorates an Act of Parliament which partially decriminalised sex between men over twenty-one in the privacy of their own homes in England and Wales. It would not become law in Scotland until 1980 and in Northern Ireland until 1982. I have not attempted to cover the entire history of LGBT+ representation in Britain over the past century. Rather, I wanted, predominantly, to examine the gay male experience. The world leading up to the 1967 Act and the years which have followed, tracing the extraordinary progress that's been made, but from a variety of unexpected angles.

Anti-gay legislation in the modern era really began with the passing of the Criminal Law Amendment Act of 1885, the so-called 'Labouchere Amendment', prohibiting 'gross indecency between males'. This became known almost at once as 'the blackmailer's charter' and was the law that ensnared Oscar Wilde. Wilde seemed an obvious place to start the monologues, but as I wanted to encompass the century, perhaps it could be from the perspective of someone with a memory of Oscar Wilde? Perhaps someone on the railway platform that infamous day he was taken to Reading Gaol? From this sprang the idea of Perce, a stretcher-bearer in the trenches of World War One and a love that almost spoke its name…

Though the series, as I've said, was to reflect mostly the gay male experience, I did want to include some female perspectives. I discovered the extraordinary story of Lillias Irma Valerie Arkell-Smith – known as Colonel Barker – who had

lived as a man, even going so far as to marry a woman. I
thought this could be the basis of a fascinating story and from it,
Jackie Clune wove *The Perfect Gentleman* and its unexpected
take on the notion of masculinity.

What was it like to be a black gay man in the past? Although
there was a thriving 'queer' demi-monde in America in the
twenties and thirties, it only seems to have touched the fringes
of the jazz scene in this country. It was astonishing, in fact, to
discover how little is known about black gay sub-culture at that
time. I re-read the biography of the artist Glyn Philpot and
thought there might be something interesting in the notion of
being an 'exotic' life model at that time. This, together with the
story of Patrick Nelson – who was one of Duncan Grant's
lovers – provided Keith Jarrett with the inspiration for *Safest
Spot in Town*.

In 1957 came the Wolfenden Report. This was the beginning of
change, though it would take a further decade for the law to
actually pass. But what aspect of this period to examine? Jon
Bradfield pitched me *Missing Alice* – an idea with which I
instantly fell in love. A woman happily married to a gay man
who worries that increasing liberalisation might make him leave
her. What a lovely, simple notion. A tiny Terence Rattigan play,
as it were.

When I first moved to London I remember being invited to what
seemed to me quite a sophisticated gay party. What I'll never
forget is chatting to an elderly man, waspish, hilarious and who
lapsed into Polari at the drop of a feather boa. 'It was never the
same, you know, dear, after it was legal,' he said. 'All the fun
went out of it.' I wanted to use this as a jumping-off point, to
explore the notion that not everyone saw legalisation as a good
thing. Matthew Baldwin, who had already co-written a
fascinating play about '67 called *The Act*, was the natural
choice to write *I Miss the War*.

With the eighties, the shadow of AIDS, of course, looms, as
monolithic as those tombstone TV ads we grew so used to. This
was the time in which I grew up as a gay man. But how to
approach this period and this subject which might feel like it's

prey to cliché? Happily, Brian Fillis came up with *More Anger* about a young gay actor who finds the health crisis affecting him in unexpected ways.

By 1994, change was in the air and the House of Commons voted to lower the homosexual age of consent. I was there that night as big crowds gathered to hear the – as it turned out, disappointing – result. Michael Dennis was also there – though we didn't know each other at the time. His memories of that experience and of being a young man enjoying the big city for the first time became *A Grand Day Out*.

Finally, *Something Borrowed* brings us – almost – to the present day and the preparations for a wedding. I wanted to celebrate this amazing state of affairs, unthinkable just a short time ago, but also to explore what might have got lost along the way. The notion of being different, an outsider, other; that illicit thrill I felt watching *If* all those years ago. Gareth McLean's monologue asks some tough questions without providing easy answers.

As we see every day, hard-won victories can be undone with the stroke of a presidential pen. Homosexuality remains illegal in seventy-four countries. In thirteen of them, it is punishable by death. But let's not forget how far we have come. And that we stand on the shoulders of giants.

Curating and directing *Queers* has been a wonderful journey, and I'd like to thank everyone involved – from the BBC to the writers, the actors, the crew and the publishers – for making it an unforgettable experience.

London, 2017

the man on the platform

mark gatiss

First performed by **Ben Whishaw**
on screen, as part of the BBC Studios production *Queers*
on BBC Four,
and by **Jack Derges**
on stage at The Old Vic, London, on 28 July 2017.

1917.

A pleasingly dark, wood-panelled pub like The Salisbury in St Martin's Lane, London.

Among the clientele we find PERCE, *thirties, sad-eyed, in a serge soldier's uniform with a Red Cross armband, alone.*

As he speaks, the other pub regulars fade away...

Douglas Fairbanks there thinks he's in with a chance, bit of company on a wet Friday night. Except old Dougie doesn't have a cast in his eye and a built-up shoe.

Least not last time I was at the flickers.

It's always the eyes. That's how you know. A glance held just that little bit too long. Dragged off to one side, like the trail of a Verey light in the dark. After the do, the interview, the officer asks me – not unkindly, I must say. He says, 'How do you chaps... chaps like you and the Captain... know one another?' So I told him. Not my words. Something somebody said to me once. 'A certain liquidity of the eye.'

That's how *he* knew.

Fade.

My eyes are bad, mind you. Too bad for shooting Prussians, at any rate. So I was shunted onto hospital work. 'Cushy,' says Sam, 'That's a charabanc holiday, Perce. You always wanted to see France, didn't you?'

I remember my first day in resus – resuscitation tent. That's where they take the dying or the nearly dying and the shocked ones. There's heated beds to put some life back into them and transfusions.

Our guns were going hell for leather. The sky was all lit up. Powdery. Green. Horrible green. Like the air was sick. Star shells. Vereys. Dumps going up.

And then the ambulances come in and we have to ferry them in, the ones that can't walk. And they've got these labels on them that tell you what's wrong with them. Like left luggage.

You ever carried a stretcher? Bloody horrible. You feel like your arms are going to pop out of their sockets. Some chaps can get very heavy.

Those that *can* walk into the hospital are covered in mud and salt sweat, caked in it. All cracked and stiff. Like moving statues. Like those poor fuckers in Pompeii what got covered in lava. I seen photographs of them in the lending library.

And then, in the resus tent, the thing you'd never expect – silence. Not a moan or a groan. They're beyond all that, most of them. Smoking. Breathing. Just about. Mind you, I've seen what a transfusion can do and it is a bloody miracle. Lads with one foot in the grave and their pulses all thready. They have the transfusion, they're up, they're joking, they're having a smoke in a couple of hours. I said to Captain Leslie, I said, 'You wouldn't credit it, would you? It's like witchcraft.' 'Sounds about right,' he says, 'since we're in hell.' But he says it with a smile. And when he does that, there's little creases in his cheeks, like ripples in the sand. 'You're a credit to this unit, Percy,' he says to me. 'You've all the tenderness of a woman.' And he shakes my hand. 'It's Terence,' he says. I say, 'What is?' He says, 'Me. My name. Terence Leslie. Do call me Terence. I can't bear all this formal rot.'

But he's an officer and it don't seem right so I'll stick to 'Captain Leslie', I say, 'if it's all the same.' He just smiles again and shrugs. His eyelashes are long. Long and blond. I can't see much of his hair because it's under his cap. But then, one day, I'm bringing in a stretcher, and he takes his hat off and, just like that, his hair tumbles out. Yellow as corn. And I must have stared because he grins at me and pushes his hair out of his eyes and says, 'Come along, Perce, stir your stumps.' But I don't move.

And just for a bit – well, like I said, held just a moment too long.

He glances towards his unseen admirer.

Douglas Fairbanks over there will give me a wink in a minute.

Beat.

There you go.

Fade.

Always been a skinny bugger, me. Thin as a whip, Mother says.
Father was the same. Mother always had a bit more beef on her
after she had Albert and me. And there was one before us. A
boy. But he died. He was called Percy an' all. Poison berries.
Never think a thing like that can happen but it does. I can
remember Mother showing me the pictures in the medicine
book. All shiny and glossy pictures like Jesus in the book at
Sunday school. And little Percy, he'd grabbed a handful of these
berries and that was that. Box, I think, the berries. Black, like
little bullets or liquorice sweeties. Maybe that's what Percy
thought they was. Anyway, they done for him. And then, a year
or so after that, along comes I. And they called me Percy too.
Bit odd, some might say, a bit morbid. But Mother always said
that she could see him in me. And she looked so funny when
she says that to me. She looked so sad.

But I don't think it's just because of little Percy because there
was another time she looked at me the same way.

Beat.

It was freezing, I remember that. We was waiting for a train.
Dad had some business in Reading. I forget what it was. We
were to come with and make a day of it. I was fifteen,
thereabouts, Albert was twelve. I'd been despatched in search of
tea and buns.

They all sat in the waiting room, steam coming off them, like
wet dogs. Anyway, I'm on my way to the refreshments and
there's a commotion. So I think, oh, the train must be coming

in. So, I say to the girl behind the tea-stall – pretty girl, I remember, with bows in her hair – I ask her to get a shift on. She says, 'What's the hurry? The Reading train's not in for another quarter of an hour.' So I think, what's all the fuss about then? And then I see it ahead of me on the platform. Policemen. At least I think they're policemen. But then I look properly and they're not. They're from the jail. Dark uniforms. Little hats with shiny brims. And between them – a, well, a prisoner, waiting to be taken away, I suppose. And it's not the first time I've seen as such. Used to see them a lot, poor bastards, shuffling along in their chains and the arrows on their clothes. And it's rough clobber too. Like to make you itch...

He fingers the collar of his uniform.

...worse than this. So why are all these folk whispering and pointing, I wonder? So I look at the chap in the chains. And he's a big chap, sort of like a, a big bear of a fellow with a big, slack, pouchy face. Fattish, except it's all sunk in now. And his hair, what was most likely black as your hat is all shot through with grey. And he looks... wretched. As well he might. There's rain dripping off his hair and down the creases in his big face. And then I realise it's not just rain, he's bloody crying. And then he looks at me. And there it was. In that moment. 'A certain liquidity of the eye.' And then he looks back down at his boots. And it's as if all the whole world has come tumbling down around him.

I stand there and I think, *he knows me*. He knows me for what I am. He can see it in me. And I start to shake. And it's not from the cold, it's shame. And fear. And... terror. Then someone starts laughing.

And there's a little girl and she's wandered close to the prisoner. She's got a little wooden horse on a bit of dirty string. And then her mother goes up and drags the girl away from the man as if he were like to eat her up.

Then I hear it. A name. Whispered behind fancy gloves and November hands what are stiff with cold. And it's *him*, isn't it? And suddenly Dad's beside me and he's gripping my arm. And he says, 'Are you alright, Perce?' And he's proper worried. And there's a sort of ringing noise in my ear and I feel for a moment like I might faint. But then this chap goes straight up to the prisoner on the platform and he… he spits in his face.

And Dad looks shocked. And just then the train comes puffing into the station, steam everywhere. And I look back to the prisoner but he's covered now in a great big cloud of steam. Dad picks up the tea and the buns and he gets us into the carriage. It smells of damp wool and musty like church. And there's beads of rain on the window, the open window. And Mother pulls down the leather strap and the sound sort of snaps me out of it.

'What was all that fuss about there, Clem?' And Dad sups at his tea and it hangs in little drops from the ends of his Kitchener 'tache. 'You won't believe it,' he says. 'Out there on the platform, waiting to be taken to prison.' 'Who?' pipes up Albert.

And he looks at us and he shakes his head in wonder. 'Oscar Wilde,' he says.

PERCE *stares into space*.

And then Mum looks at me – tender, like.

Beat.

I've never had the nerve. That's the thing, I suppose. The notion of getting in trouble or being a bother. I could always imagine Mother's face if she'd found out I'd been… up to things. And I couldn't bear it, I couldn't bear to disappoint.

So I didn't, I didn't do anything about it. Not even a tuppeny wank with Sam or nothing. I kept me own counsel, as they say.

Also there was a girl who was sweet on me, Annie. And that sort of stopped people asking, I suppose. We courted for a long while but then she got fed up because I never asked her to marry me. I took on like Annie'd broke me heart. And then, what with one thing or another, and then the war, it sort of, somehow I got away with it. A lot of questions, of course, especially when all us Tommies was billeted together for the first time. 'You married?' 'No.' 'You got a girl?' 'Well, I used to…'

And then, one day, in Amiens, there was a sort of lull. Hot as hell, it was. Not what you think. People think of all that mud and rain. But we was there the live-long year. And sometimes it was hot and parched. Fucking flies everywhere. Blue and green bellies on them. Fat. Great clouds of them because of the dead bodies. And Captain Leslie comes up to me and he slaps me on the shoulder and he says, 'Come along, Perce, we're going hunting!' And I say, 'What?' And he says, 'Butterflies!' Because we were camped on sort of downland. And there's marigolds and poppies all over with little splashes of colour. I can still taste the dust. Chalky. In your mouth and your hair and on the Dunlop tyres like white paint, because Terence had only gone and got us bicycles, the silly bugger!

And it was only for a few hours but you could forget, you know, for a bit, everything that was going on. And we came to this sort of lake. It was a crater-hole, I suppose, and the water was glass-green and clear like a perfume bottle. And Terence, he starts hollering and rattling the bike down to the water and he pulls off all his clothes and in he goes! I follows. And then we go splashing about in our birthday suits. And he's brick-red from the sunshine, but not where his shirt's been so he's got this sort of red face and arms but the rest of him is… is like a ghost.

And after we've swum about we just lie on the grass and fall asleep. You can hear the buzz of the flies, but they're a way off and some of the ones that are closer ones are butterflies so that's alright. And I just lie there and I watch Terence sleeping and his Adam's apple bobbing up and down. And his hair is golden and the line of his jaw is just sort of… perfect. Like a draughtsman's drawn it. Like *I'd* drawn it. And his lips are dark and full and they're like bramble. And all I want to do is bend down and…

And he opens his eyes and squints. Then he lifts his hand to cover them so he can see better. And he says, 'We'd best be getting back.'

Beat.

We all had on us the stench of death. The bread we ate, the stagnant water. Everything we touched had a rotten smell. But that day everything was okay. It was bright. And it was pure, you see. And nobody had seen, had they?

Fade.

I done my bit. The officer mentioned that, exemplary service. When he took me aside for a quiet word. And, of course, what had Terence and me, what had the Captain and me – got up to? Sweet F.A. But someone had seen us they thought, 'Hello, what's going on here?' And it's bad for morale and all that. So I was to be sent elsewhere.

And of course I didn't get to see the Captain, did I, because he'd been transferred too.

I was packed onto this carriage, sweat and tobacco smelling and fellas pushing up against you and shoving for room. And the train gives a great big lurch and then it starts off. I just sit down on the floor and pull me cap over me eyes and I drift off.

I don't know how much time has passed, but I wake up and it's dark outside. And the train's pulling into a station.

And in the carriage it's just these little night lights on, bluey. Make everyone looks three-parts dead. And the train pulls into the station. And it's going slow like, puffing like some of them boys in the resus tent. And then... I *do* see him. Terence. He's out the window, on the platform. Greatcoat, hair tucked under his cap, neat. And he's talking to someone and they must have made him laugh because there's those little lines in his cheeks again. But he don't see me. So I push through the carriage past the other fellas. And it's not easy because most have dropped off and I trip over some poor bugger and he curses at me. But I make it to the window. And I pull down the sash. And the air outside is warm. And all I want to do is wave. But, of course, what can I say? 'So long, Captain Leslie.' 'So long, Perce.'

But then he does see me. He glances over but he's still talking to his pal. And just then, the train lurches forward, the brakes go on and the blue lights go out. And just like that, pitch black. And all the other fellas in the carriage start groaning and someone says, 'Oh, here we fucking go.' But all I can feel is my heart beating... and the air and the darkness pressing against the window and my hand gripping the window ledge.

And then someone takes my hand. Someone outside on the platform. And it's Terence. And he takes my hand and he just... lifts it to his lips and he kisses it.

There's no train then. There's no troops, there's no war. There's just his bramble-lips pressed against the tips of my fingers. And all the hair on my neck goes up on end...

And then the train lurches forward and he's let go of my hand – and all the blue lights go on. And outside there's nothing but steam.

Steam and darkness.

Fade to black.

the perfect gentleman

jackie clune

First performed by **Gemma Whelan**
on screen, as part of the BBC Studios production *Queers*
on BBC Four,
and on stage at The Old Vic, London, on 28 July 2017.

1929.

BOBBY *sits at a pub table. He is smoking a cigarette. He is elegantly dressed – hair sleek, perfectly groomed, upright, self-assured. Every inch the perfect gentleman.*

He glances about furtively then pulls a small pocket mirror from his jacket. Smoothes his hair. Adjusts his tie. Fiddles with a collar stud. Glances up once more before quickly adjusting his crotch.

Can I tell you something? Strictly *entre nous*?

I am not what I seem. I am not a man. That is to say, I was not born a man. But I do not wish to be a man. *No.* I like the costume, I like the ease, I like the way I am able to be in the world but I am very much (female).

Space.

A gentleman must take up space. Head erect, shoulders back, chest proud. No hint of apology. No fluttery hands or silly unnecessary gestures. One must enter the room and know that one is instantly the biggest thing in it. Expect that.

One must sit with a wide stance, knees an acre apart as much as to say, 'I am the Emperor here and you must make room for my enormous appendage.' If you'll excuse me.

Keep it under your hat, old bean. It's just our little secret. She is not what he seems. And she, as a he, can rattle around as he pleases and if he so pleases to indulge in a bout of beard-splitting, then so be it. No one will bat an eyelid and one can carry on being a cake-eater till one has had one's fill.

Did you clock it? If so, how so? I am a renowned gentleman, you know. I pass. I pass terribly well.

Although it seems not so well as I had hoped. Not when it matters.

A clock chimes.

She's late.

Fade.

I've always been outdoorsy. My poor old ma used to say, 'Ellen Mary Paige, you'll be the death of me! Get inside and scrub them knees – you look like a regular Tom!' I was always out playing. With Lizzy mostly. Up and down Mare Street, nicking whelks off the one-eyed man with the seafood stall – she'd distract him by asking for a pint of prawns and a blank stare – and I'd blindside him and pocket a fistful of cockles.

I adored Lizzy and she adored me. Every night when we dragged ourselves away from each other I'd say 'Cash or cheque?' And she'd say 'Cash' – and I'd get a kiss on the cheek. Our favourite game was Wedding Day.

It was always her idea. She was always the bride – of course – and I would be the groom. I'd get my dad's best coat – grey tweed, leather buttons, smell of sweat, coal, bits of dried-up tobacco in the breast pocket. I'd have to wait for her at the end of the aisle – the back alley where our mothers would hang the washing – and I'd watch her, holding my breath as she picked her way through the grey sheets and stained drawers, a huge stupid smile on her face. And when she reached me, and put her arm through mine, I fair exploded.

I loved her. I knew that. I longed to take her in my arms and kiss her neck. Would she allow it? Could she? I just didn't know.

Then bloody William Foyle turned up. All big muscles, crooked smile and twinkly-eyed. She fell for him straight away. He bought her a tuppence bag of aniseed balls and she was lost.

I was heartbroken. She still said 'Cash' when we did manage to see each other, but I could see her heart wasn't in it.

She looked sad – but not for her, for me. That was bloody hard to stomach. 'Don't be like that, Ellen,' she'd say, touching my arm.

Once she took me in, took pity on me. We sat by the fire. I had my arms wrapped around her waist and... I just let my hand drop lower and lower until it was resting in her glorious lap. She let it there and carried on stroking my face. It was quiet. I stopped shaking, held my breath. I moved my hand slowly, slowly. She froze. Then relaxed. I waited. Minutes groaned by.

She let me. She let me.

Suddenly she jumped up, grabbed her shawl and ran out the back door. I called after her, but she didn't turn back.

It was exactly two weeks later that I ran into her buying a loaf of bread. Her face went white as the flour on the loaf.

'Lizzie – ' I said. 'I'm sorry, please please speak to me.'

'Don't,' she said. And she sort of hissed it. 'Not here.'

I searched her face for a sign of softness, but there was none. There was only fear. Only fear.

She turned on her heel and marched off. 'Cash or cheque?' I called after her, hoping against hope to make her laugh, to bring back even for a moment our old closeness.

She didn't miss a beat.

'Cheque,' she shouted over her shoulder and disappeared into the fog.

I was sixteen. My life was over. Ellen Mary Paige was dead.

Beat.

I moved away after that. Went south of the river. Found lodgings, didn't speak to anyone or go out at all at first. I had very little money of course – only what I could make as a skivvy. I washed pots morning, noon and night. Set fires. Peeled potatoes. Bored rigid I was. But dead inside so it didn't matter.

'Is this it?' I'd think to myself.

Then one day I was told to throw some of Sir's old clothes out – apparently he was trying to become more *à la mode* and wanted only brogues and Oxford bags. I took the package up the scullery steps and opened it. Smell of old tobacco, sweat, soap. And I pressed the white dress shirt close to my face and breathed it in. Trousers too, high-waisted, black-satin trim down the legs, white-silk bow tie, long-line tuxedo, top hat – the lot. I stuffed the parcel behind the bin and waited for the end of the day and grabbed it on my way out.

That was the first night. I went home and put it all on.

It was like a sacrament.

I felt wonderful.

The second night I got daring and looked in the mirror. I must have posed for hours, tilting my head this way and that, practising my walk. I really thought I was the cat's particulars. The frog's eyebrows. The third night I got bold and went out. I couldn't look at anyone – I couldn't breathe. I was sure at any moment someone would point and laugh, shout at me, call me 'Nancy Boy'. But I am tall, and broad-shouldered, with a bosom like two bee stings. I know the gaslight helped, it was foggy, and the top hat was a touch too big – it kept falling down over my eyes.

But I was a man.

Fade.

I went out every night after that. Started going into pubs, ordering beer, sitting at the bar smoking. Plagued by no one. The odd nod from the other gents – I liked it. I started to feel – not happy but – free. Free in my misery. And the queer thing is I started to resent my maid's garments. I began to feel silly in my skirts, as if my pinny were a costume and not my tux.

Then the ladies started coming in. Just one or two, only at weekends, and always with their husbands. It wasn't difficult to spot the unhappy ones.

They'd sit sipping their gin silently, eyes cast down, fidgeting, while their men jawed on. I started to catch the attention of the odd lady. I'd smile, bow my head at them. They would blush.

One or two of the braver ones started to manufacture conversation when I passed – discreetly – the weather, the horses, things they thought a gentlemen might like to discuss. Then one night, a lady called Alice – forty, plump, sad-eyed – somewhat in her cups, grabbed my arm and asked to meet me out back.

Well, I was stumped, but waited a few minutes and followed her out. She was waiting in the shadows. She grabbed me and started babbling about how she felt a curious morbid attraction to me and needed to kiss me just once. I pressed my lips on hers and she groaned. One thing led to another and before long I was sliding my hand under her skirts every Friday night.

Others followed. Word got round about 'the Doctor of Southwark'. They said I could cure hysteria by inducing paroxysms. They would tiptoe in, and one by one I'd give them the nod and we'd go out back and I'd shuffle them off. I did six in one night one busy Saturday. I got cramp.

I've read *The Well of Loneliness*. (*Quoting*.) 'That night, they were not divided'? She should have got out more.

But I never let them touch me, even though I had started to pack myself with an old sock. Just the one – I'm not a crower.

'You're nice,' they'd say. 'You're different – the perfect gentleman.'

Then Sally came. No man.

She breezed in with a couple of other girls, egging each other on. Fresh from the meadows and longing to be led astray. She caught my eye and held it. I fell instantly in love. She was eighteen and never been kissed. But she was bold. Hungry for her life to start. And – I found – so was I. I walked her home three miles. Floated back to Southwark.

Saw her every Saturday. She was working at Boots in Piccadilly and on my day off I'd go in to make her blush. I'd ask her loudly for 'a little something for the weekend'. The other girls would laugh at me, say, 'Here he is – Burlington Bertie!' If only they knew I was more Vesta Tilley than they could ever imagine...

(*Singing*.)
'I walk down the Strand with me gloves on me 'ands
And I walk down again with them off…'

Did they know? Could they see? Sally didn't. Or didn't seem to. Or didn't want to.

Until last night. I'm such a fool. Such an utter idiot. I don't know why I thought it would ever work.

We'd been intimate for some weeks – three, four – but she wasn't like the others. She wanted more. A lot more. She said she loved me. Wanted us to go steady. I was so deliriously happy. I asked her to marry me. Marry me!? She said yes. Straight away. She didn't even want to wait.

'I want to marry you *now*, Bobby Paige! Right now! I want to wash your socks and have twelve babies and make you steak pudding and kiss you every night,' she'd say. Smothering me with her mouth, trying to pull on my flies. I managed to push her away but she only fought harder, laughing, saying why was I shy and surely a handsome chap like me had had scores of girls.

Well, she became more and more insistent. She started borrowing filthy books from a dirty puzzle of a girl at work. The language – I'd never heard the like.

'I've got standing room for one,' she'd whisper, or 'I need my chimney swept good and proper.'

It was me blushing then. But it… did things to me. I started to get nervous that she would leave me. I tried to break it off but I couldn't – I loved her.

So… I did something utterly insane. Such sheer folly.

Oh God.

And that's why I'm in this pickle. You see the big house has a lot of candles. Yesterday I was replacing the old ones in the dining room – she likes fresh every night – and it got me to thinking – 'What a waste.' Don't laugh, but I whittled one at the end – I've never seen a real one (had to avoid the urinals for obvious reasons) but I've seen Dirty Puzzle's filthy books so I had a good idea.

I stuck it in my underwear. It kept slipping out. Quite a queer gait I had walking down the street. But I liked it.

I went to pick her up from work, waited round the back. As soon as she saw me she grabbed me and kissed me. Pushed me up against the bins. Fumbled for my privates – and I let her. She smiled. Reached for my flies and let out a gasp.

And then she pulled up her skirts and said, 'Stick it in me.' Just like that. It was dark. Cold. 'Why not?' thought I. 'Why not?'

So we did it. And after she said, 'Thank you,' and looked so pleased. I could have died happy, her clinging on to me, her hot breath on the back of my neck as she calmed herself.

And then it fell out. Slipped out of my hand and then my trousers. She screamed. For a moment I think she thought she'd broken it. But then she saw… what it was… and her face… it… folded in on itself. And she gathered up her skirts and ran.

I mean… how can she not have known? Surely… a candle… It's just… the wrong kind of stiff.

I don't think I can do this any more.

Then this morning a note… 'Who are you? What are you?'

> (*Singing*.)
> 'I'm Bert, p'raps you've heard of me
> Bert, you've had word of me,
> Jogging along, hearty and strong
> Living on plates of fresh air
> I dress up in fashion
> And when I am feeling depressed
> I shave from my cuff all the whiskers and fluff
> Stick my hat on and toddle up west…'

The bell rings as the pub door opens.

BOBBY *looks up – and beams.*

Fade to black.

safest spot in town

keith jarrett

First performed by **Kadiff Kirwan**
on screen, as part of the BBC Studios production *Queers*
on BBC Four,
and on stage at The Old Vic, London, on 31 July 2017.

1941.

The all-clear siren sounds, and FREDRICK *– twenty-five, dandy-ish, dressed formally, but in bright colours – stumbles through the door. He looks shocked and his mouth is bleeding.*

I require a drink – that… that is for certain. I'll be seen here though. Someone will bring up my name and say, 'Isn't that Andrew's boy standing over there?' Andrew's boy.

He hisses.

You'd think this was a bush village.

Bush village – that way. Soho, Bloomsbury, Piccadilly Circus, full of clowns. Everything else is either slum or pompous, and little in between. I know what I'm saying. I've run the length of this city so I know it all. All of it… the East End too.

And I don't just mean cruising up and down Whitechapel High Street like those old queans do. No, I mean down by the docks. Workers from around the world with big load-lifting arms – oh my God. If their overalls could speak, they'd shame up the whole of polite society. There's the Chinese and people from the West Indies and more. And the locals, of course. Hmm, hands as rough as Empire.

But down over there, you're never far from an alleyway and a poof-rorting. Yes, that's what they call them here – *poof-rorters* – the men who might just as well leave you for dead afterwards. That's after they've taken their pleasure. The beating come and your money go. Threats to involve the law, if they believe you have a reputation worth looking out for. No, the East End is not for me. Uh-huh.

What is for me is much harder to fathom. This mess of dance halls, theatres, smoke-filled bars and endless gossip that draws me in, holds me close. This bush village.

Three years ago, almost to the day, when I first come here. Southampton Docks was where I first arrived, all sea-legged and smiley. I thought I knew it all. I thought I knew all there was to know about the Motherland and daffodils and all the poets from the Great War. I thought I knew what to expect. My daddy told me about the way cold here creeps into your fingers and toes until your bones weep. He talked me to death about the English cricket teams. He packed me a bat and some knee pads and told me, off you go: 'If you cyaan be a sportsman like me, best you get yourself a proper degree. Come back with a profession. Make yourself into a lawyer or a doctor and don't bring no shame on we.' And that was that, I was free.

I was almost twenty-two and unmarried. No profession but more than good enough grades to get me into a law school. But I didn't want law school over there – and I didn't really want it here either. What I wanted – what I still want – is much harder to fathom. But it don't look like a wife or a briefcase.

Fade.

1938, yes, and what a time to arrive. I had the spring and summer to myself. I saw Cornwall, Wales, Scotland, countryside, all kinds of people I didn't understand. I saw poor *white* people for the first time. A white man trundling along with a broom sweeping the streets. White men begging. Old white men with sunken eyes, still lost from a war they'd fought two decades before. I was confused. My father never tell me about all of that.

In Wales, I became a valet for a gentleman. Oh his poor wife. If she ever knew the things we did behind her back. My daddy's knee pads come in handy, I tell you. But Wales was not for long. London was my calling. When I come back here, I made a few shillings as an artists' model, standing naked and still while this city ran around me, painting me all different shades of wrong. At some point though I stopped looking at the finished work when the artists called me round to the other side of the easel. Sometimes it's best to keep your eyes closed while keeping your eyes open.

I started moving with the bohemians in Bloomsbury. They were all painters and writers and rabble-rousers and hangers-on – and I was adopted into their crowd. Their *Freddy*. I don't remember all the names. But the bedposts I can describe in great detail. Four-posters, some of them. Or sometimes a *chaise longue* in the middle of a studio. Tiny little rooms with laughing floorboards. We'd have late nights drinking at the bottle parties. Those places – places like The Shim Sham – where you had someone other than your shadow to dance with.

You could press another man to you, hold him close, feel him stiffen against your hips and then... release. You had to glide with the music, you see. That's unless some *asterbar* had called for the police, in which case, when you heard the footsteps raining down, you took the hand of the nearest lady. It was a fluid movement. Then there were the soirees and what they called dalliances between three or more of us. And it was just then, just as I was going to think about my studies, in amongst all of them, in the middle of a room, there he is. *Andrew*. As sweet and as dizzy-making as an entire bottle of Wray & Nephew rum.

He's over twice my age on paper but there is that something in my blood that draws the sweet and complicated to me. He has this wicked grin, a posterior like one of those marble statues I used to go visit at the British Museum. Thighs you'd want to hold on to for years. He painted me into his life. He carried me into his studio and we did not leave it for a month. And then... and then...

I remember seeing myself in one of his watercolours on a wall in a gallery in Belgravia and I couldn't help thinking to myself, why he paint me so dark, eenh? I remember standing there with my hand up to the wall and my arm and contrasting it. He had me down just right. He had me down so right he could paint me without me being there.

And, after a while, I was not there so much. Some part of me will always remain on that wall, I imagine, in a gold-leaf frame. The other part of me needs to move on, could never really stick itself to a white canvas. I don't want to waste my youth stuck to the wall of his imagination. He though, he'd rather keep me there. We write to each other still, making promises to meet that are rarely kept.

I distract myself as much as I can with the theatre. I've been tending to the theatre, my personal back garden, even though it's one bomb after another, one bomb after another. Even though all the places for inverts like me are disappearing one by one, there is still so much sweet for all that bitter.

This beer is far too weak for my taste, but it will do the trick. It's one for the road and it tastes like tarmac too.

Monday things must change. My free paper burn but I still have tomorrow to dance.

A distant bomb blast causes a shower of dust to fall in front of FREDRICK *and he looks upwards.*

Fade.

I have 'Dodging a Divorcee' in my head and I can't shake it out.

I wish I could carry that song with me everywhere I go – press it against my ears.

If only! If only. It's a foxtrot. No foxtrot now but they're playing ragtime in the ballrooms. *Ragtime.* All those West Indians giving the crowd what they want: sweating, smiling, shuffling colonial boys. It's all a part of the game of belonging and not belonging.

When I first come over here, the landlady was full of questions: 'Why are your palms a lighter hue?' She'd turn them over at the table, frowning in puzzlement. I let it wash over me like the other questions: 'Where'd you learn to speak such good English then?' and the like. She was full of them. I used to think it was a working-class obsession, my skin, my hair, the colour of my hands. All those comments from the East End boys. But I'm under no illusions now. The more refined have their ways. I tell them I'm going to become a lawyer and their eyebrows arch. I talk to them about music and the conversation moves to jiving,

swing and ragtime. All that time I spent revelling in the
attention of that Bloomsbury crowd. The freedom I felt was an
illusion. I know that now. Where I was born, you have to be as
light as cornmeal to succeed, unless you know how to entertain.
Here is more complicated, an endless game of where you're
schooled and who you know.

Oh, they never slam a door in your face, the upper classes here.
No, they make you hold the handle of the door and convince
you that you don't want to come in after all. But all of that is
changing with this blasted war. Tonight I was good enough for
the Café de Paris because there was no one else left in Soho.

The grand Café de Paris is where you can dance now. Where I
can dance now. They're no longer concerned with my
appearance. They started opening up their clientele, that's what
they said. It's funny how some places changed their tune, eenh?
They call it the safest spot in town. Deep underground, with a
full swing band. A West Indian band at that, a whole heap of
brass and brown skins. Who would have thought that, eenh?

Fade.

I was going tonight. To the Café de Paris. To go see Snakehips,
the king of swing, the bandleader at the helm of it all. He has a
twinkle in his eye, this hypnotising movement at the loins that
make a boy like me salivate. He was like that from day one,
Snakehips, before he pluck himself out from among the riff-raff
to make it into the big halls. They all talk about him, Snakehips.
Even the Thames seem to do a little dancing dip like he does,
once the river hits this side of town. But all that he do isn't real
music, it's all showmanship. And I'm not complaining – though
one entertains, the other sustains. And it's not that I don't like
the swing, the way it makes your body bend. But that is the real
difference between the bottle parties and the Café de Paris. It's
not just who gets past the doors but what's behind them.

I could have been hit by that bomb tonight. I should be dead. I
didn't go there tonight. I went – I went to the *theatre*. That's
what I call it, the lavatories around Piccadilly where men who

speak my language like to entertain each other. The *real* West End theatres are all closed now. Soon after the bombs started coming they were forced to. But the Café de Paris was open for business. Too deep underground for the Germans to hit it.

I was meant to go but I couldn't bring myself to darken the doors of a place that would have refused me entry just a year ago. I'm too proud for that. Nobody ever tell me in words but I feel it in the tailoring of my skin. Well, proud or weak-hearted, the result is the same. I wasn't good enough to enter then, unless I was one of the entertainers.

I was on my way and then this urge came upon me like a river and my feet meandered away from the entrance of the club and straight into the theatre inside the Regent's Palace Hotel. It was a fluid movement. The porters often turn a blind eye, so long as we don't cause a disturbance. I was stood at the urinals, in the semi-dark, with a middle-aged man's hands inside my flies. And he had a strong grip too.

Halfway through, the sirens went off and we had to run for shelter right away. All of us, except for the chancers, as always. The chance of a few minutes to find a hand or mouth or more in the dark is too good to pass by.

I escaped into the street and I caught a glint in the eye of a warden, and I followed him down a side passage. He tasted of the suburbs, like he had a Hammersmith wife waiting for him at the back of his throat. There's that something in my blood that draws the married man to me, with all his sweetness and complications. It's not a bad thing; I have a sweet tooth.

He catches himself laughing.

Oh, Snakehips is in my head still. Boy, he could move.

I heard the whistle of it landing and I could feel the ground around me shake as I pulled the warden's thighs close against me.

I can see Snakehips dancing – and I can hear him singing… right as the bomb lifted him clean off the stage.

The bomb went down the ventilation shaft and then… boom!

The safest spot in London, gone just like that. It was an hour or two ago now, but here we are drinking on.

Another one went off ten minutes later, while I still have the taste of the warden in my mouth. And just as I'm arriving to the shelter there's all this debris falling and I don't know where the blood come from, if I hit my head or bit my lip too hard, but all I see is blood.

I could have been there. I promised myself I would finally see inside of that blessèd club, take my rightful place with the crème de la crème. But sometimes a broken promise is what it takes to keep you alive.

Instead, I chose the path of the warden who tasted of Hammersmith and gin. I can't have been more than two hundred yards away from where the bomb hit and I survived.

Monday – Monday is the day I'm going to join up for war service. I'll join up before I'm forced to, in my way, in the Fredrick way. And I will survive same way, like I've always done.

Of course I knew one day I'll be called up. I dreaded it. I never wanted it. I'd rather dance away my days than join in the bloodshed. But tonight, *tonight* I finally realised that the fight will come to me if I don't come to it first. And I will fight for this bush village. For the bottle parties that have come and gone, for the sweet and complicated men that have come and gone. And yes, for Snakehips. And yes, for the Café de Paris. But also for the theatres. Most of all, I'm going to fight for the theatres and all the other places that never close their doors to men like me. That's if they even have doors to start with. That is the only fight I can take up with any conviction.

And I will be back some time and I will sit down in a Soho pub, which will be better than here. And maybe even better than The Shim Sham. And God help them if they haven't learned to pour decent beer by then.

Fade to black.

missing alice

jon bradfield

First performed by **Rebecca Front**
on screen, as part of the BBC Studios production *Queers*
on BBC Four,
and by **Sara Crowe**
on stage at The Old Vic, London, on 31 July 2017.

1957.

ALICE, *forty-seven, sits in her coat and nurses a drink. She used to be working class, but is now more middle class. She's good-humoured with a slightly non-conformist edge.*

I've had two babies, you see. If you're counting. I was sixteen, the first one. A boy from our street was the father, though that's a bloody grown-up word for a boy that age. Course he couldn't marry me, he had an uncle who'd made good in Cardiff as an undertaker and was going to train him up. Dad said, 'Well, he can probably be trusted with dead bodies.' Mum didn't like that. I didn't see the point in coming up with a name for her.

Dad asked the man at the Home and Colonial to take me on, as I'd best earn a living. Mum said, 'Men don't like damaged goods.' Well, they won't if you call them damaged goods. I liked it at the shop, all the foods.

After I'd had the baby, Mum made me sit at the back in church, away from the family to show she was taking our collective shame seriously. And that's where I met Michael. They were a bit posh his family, well, compared to the rest of the congregation. Not posh compared to what I met after through Michael, you know. He was new at church. A bit older, but he took to sitting at the back with me so he could make jokes. Not to shock me – he knew I was hardly a nun.

Michael didn't believe in God but he liked the singing. I used to laugh at his singing. 'Do I sing funny?' he asked. 'No,' I said. 'You sing lovely, that's what's funny.' I says to him he should be in the choir, but he said he liked sitting with me and that you can't muck about if you're in the choir. 'Or,' he said, 'in the case of this choir, sing in bloody tune.' Two months after he first set eyes on me, he asked me to marry him. I didn't see it coming. Not because of my scandal. It just hadn't occurred. He was me pal. We had a laugh. And it was his little brother Charlie I'd got me eye on. Charlie. He'd just started in the police, and he had such thick dark hair he always looked like he hadn't shaved since yesterday. He's gone to seed now, Charlie, like some men do.

Dad said it was up to me if I married Michael. Mum said, 'How soon can you do it?' I just thought, 'Well, Alice, it could be fun.'

She smiles.

It was his parents got us the weekend in Brighton. We got in the hotel room and the curtains were shut tight, even though it was broad daylight outside. 'I think they're dropping hints!' I said. Michael seemed not to hear that and went and straightened a picture on the wall. I sat on the bed. And there was a vase of little flowers on the bedside table so I took one out and put it between me lips like I'm some sort of, well, I don't know... Only cos of the dark I hadn't realised the flowers were made of bloody cloth so I'm sat there all demure spitting fluff and dust out my mouth. He laughed at that, we both did, so I patted the bed beside me like this...

She pats her thigh.

But he didn't seem to... Well, I thought you were meant to get straight to it, see, what with how people bang on about honeymoons with their winks and nudges. I say people – silly girls who wouldn't know sex from tobogganing. Michael looks me up and down like he's taking me in. And he says, 'That bedspread is the same pattern as your dress.' He goes to the window and opens the curtains. It wasn't a sea view, but he stands there anyway, peering outside with all the specks of dust swarming round his head. He must be nervous, I thought.

That'll be it. That's what I thought. Well, he'd probably not done it before and, of course, he knew I had. So I said, 'Come on, let's go out.' Out of the hotel, I mean. We had supper, and went dancing at one of the smarter ones on the front which had palm trees and a band. He's a lovely mover, is Michael. When the band stopped we were both half-cut – well, half is an understatement. So we stumbled back, fell into bed and passed out. The second night, he said he felt sick.

Fade.

We lived with Helen and Jack at first. That's Michael's mum
and dad. Oh, they treated me nice, but I looked forward to him
coming home of a night. I'd stopped working at the Home and
Colonial, see, cos Mr Barrett didn't think it right for a married
woman to stay on. Michael would come in eight, nine, even ten
sometimes, bit of supper, game of cards. He said he was funny
about sex, what with his mum and dad sleeping only in the next
room. So, I'd lie there with him breathing next to me, gentle
enough, and his dad snoring like heavy artillery from through
the wall. Well, it was only for a few weeks.

Now, when we got our flat – well, you shoulda seen it, Mum's
face. Helen and Jack had helped us out you see so it was, you
know.

Michael got this young handyman he'd met in a pub to come
round and put up a big new mirror in our bedroom. Came round
in the day when Michael was at work. Nice-looking chap he
was, all strong in his rolled-up sleeves. And his shoulders when
he lifted the thing up – I'd to stop myself saying something. He
wouldn't stay for a cup of tea after, he had more calls to make…
As he left he stopped in the door to bid me 'Good day, ma'am,'
and said would I thank my nice husband for him.

When he'd gone, I stood looking in the mirror. The room
seemed twice the size. I took my clothes off, all of them. I don't
know why. Curtains were open and everything, dress and
petticoat on the floor. Come on, Alice, let's have a look at you. I
can get fat… if I'm not careful. Fat on my hips and arms and on
my neck and it doesn't look nice on me like with some women.
Course it was natural, with me not being on my feet all day in
the shop no more, but all I could think was, well, *I* wouldn't
fuck me.

Well, it's easily solved, innit? You eat less.

One night – this is five, six months later – he comes home late
as ever. He's a few drinks inside him and he's got this new
briefcase, proper shiny chestnut job with gold fasteners. A
present he says. 'Did work give you that?' He says, 'No, it was
from a friend.' 'You've got nice friends,' I said. 'I have,' he

said, sort of proud and sheepish at the same time. A few weeks later, it was cufflinks. He was pleased as punch with them till he realised he didn't have any of the right sort of shirts with holes in.

And when he came home the next night, I was waiting for him. 'Is it a woman bought you those presents?' He shakes his head. Sits down on the arm of the armchair, which his mum always told him off for doing because it puts the frame out of shape. 'It's not a woman,' he says. He puts his head in his hands. 'It's not women.'

She smiles and shakes her head.

I knew right away what he meant. It was like the room shifted. Like when they cut to a different angle in a film scene, or like how everything seems to settle different after you step off a carousel. So I go from feeling fat to feeling bloody stupid. He looks more surprised than me that he's said it. I tell him, I can't be your wife, can I? He looked surprised at that too. You know what he said? 'I'd miss you, Alice. I'd miss you.'

Fade.

The next week, Helen invites me to lunch. Well, I can hardly say I'm too busy. She gives me a hug right there in the porch. She's more – oh what's the word – demonstrative than Mum is, and you go along with it, but this time it's verging on assault. She says we'll eat in the kitchen, it's less formal. Well, it's also the only room in the house that's properly warm so it suits me well enough. On the table there's a bottle of wine. 'I know it's lunch but I thought we'd be naughty,' she says. 'It's a good one apparently so don't tell my husband.' Calm down, love, I wasn't thinking to leave him a note. She's done us chops with cauliflower cheese which she knows I like. 'How's the flat?' 'Nice, thank you.' Her napkin's fallen off her lap onto the floor three times so she gives up on it and puts it on the table instead, clenched in her hand. And then she comes out with it. 'You're having trouble,' she says. 'It's not me with the trouble,' I say. 'We know how Michael is,' she says. Oh.

It sounds stupid but it is really bothering me that the woman has somehow got cheese sauce on her wrist and she hasn't noticed and I now can't mention it cos it's not quite the moment. 'It doesn't mean he can't be a good husband to you,' she says. 'Better that than drink, or gambling, or illness… or women.' Thing is – and this is God's own truth – I don't give a monkey's what he gets up to elsewhere but… well, what I say to her is, if it was women at least he might show *me* some interest too.

Bugger it, I'm close to crying, but I don't. She reaches out her hand to me and before she can touch me, thank God, she finally notices the muck on her wrist. 'He's very fond of you,' she says. 'And so are we.' And then – and this is my mother-in-law – and then she says, 'If that's all that's missing, can't you just pretend everything is normal, and if you have needs occasionally I'm sure if you're careful you can go elsewhere.'

They'll look after me well, she says. I'll have a good life. She says I won't have forgotten how his brother's a policeman and it would all be very difficult for him if word got out, and how surely after my own mishap I of all people know how important it is to appear respectable.

I walk home, hour and a half even though the wind's up. I can't face the Tube. When Michael gets in, nearly midnight it is, he sees my face and he looks like he's just watched his own death. 'I'm so sorry,' he says. 'It wasn't my idea.' I just run at him, hitting him in the chest over and over and over until I crumple and he holds me tight. 'You got so bloody skinny,' he says. He asks, will I let him make me tea and put me to bed, and in the morning I can think what I want to do and he will help me, whatever I decide. Well, I don't have anywhere else to go, that I'd want to go.

We don't say a word until I'm in bed. I'm shattered. He gets in too, I don't stop him. And then, in the dark and safe with my back to him, I say, 'It was your brother I always fancied.' He snorts into my neck. 'Yeah, you and half of London,' he says.

He puts an arm round me, his hand warm and flat on my tummy… like he sometimes does. A minute later, he's cupping my breast. Usually he stays well clear, but no mistake. It feels electric. He shuffles himself up close behind me so I can feel that he's hard. My heart's bloody pounding so loud I can hear it. I keep my eyes shut even though it's dark and I can hear the clock ticking from his side of the bed, slower than my heart's beating, everything out of pace. But it's nice.

His hand slides back down from my breast to my stomach. And further down, until he finds me. And his mouth is hot on my neck. I don't respond to any of it – until I do. So now we were what you call properly husband and wife. A month later, the doctor tells me I'm to start feeding myself properly. And that I'm pregnant.

Fade.

ALICE *smiles at someone.*

That's Salim over there, just come in. The Arab-looking one. Obviously. He's very charming. Not unflirtatious with me either, considering he usually walks in here with one man and leaves with another. I'll say hello in a minute. He'll ask what I'm doing in here by myself. He's very direct you see, with his being foreign. In here without Michael, is what he'll mean. Well, why not? It's as much my pub as his these days, in a way. Especially since Violet moved out and that's, God, nearly ten years. Can you believe it?

Violet – that's our daughter. When she was a couple of years old, I suggested to Michael he might bring friends over more often, if he wanted. Friends or… you know. Better that than not seeing him. Better that than nights in without him.

He was shy about it at first – he'd always been very discreet, you couldn't fault him. But we soon had men about. Still do. They come over, one or more of them, play cards, have a few drinks. He does very well for himself, Michael. He didn't go to seed like his brother, see. I don't know how he finds them. Well, who cares?

I should go. I only came into town to buy theatre tickets for his birthday. I know, *fancy*. Me and him and Tony – he's Michael's current friend. Been a few weeks now, older than he usually goes for, more settled, you know. Then Violet and her fella – oh, and a couple we're friendly with, George and Pierre. Pierre's not French, he's from Carlisle. He said to me once, he said, 'Alice, me and George is just like any other normal long-time couple – we ain't had it off in years. At least, not with each other.'

Last Friday, it was, in the afternoon when I found out it had become a, how would you say it, an appropriate subject for public discussion. Tony came round, Michael's Tony – he'd left his wallet at ours. Michael was at work. And Tony puts a newspaper article into my hands that he's cut out. 'What do you make of this, Alice?' The Report on Homosexual Offences. The headline's just three words: 'Crime and Sin'. 'Imagine that, Alice,' he says. 'Two men being allowed to do what they like, legal. No pretending.' And he goes.

But you see, for Michael it's not like with George and Pierre. They can do what they like. George is an actor and Pierre cuts ladies' hair. Michael's got a respectable job. It's been nice for him, having a wife, having a family. Anyway, even if things were legal – normal, even – he wouldn't want to go off and live all 'happy-couples' with a man. Not at his age. Not at *our* age. It wouldn't make him happier, would it. He's got all he needs, always has, hasn't he.

Well. This was Friday like I say so it's cinema night and we were going to see *The Bridge Over the River Kwai*. It was very good actually – it's our sort of film. We don't go for the romantic ones, though there's usually a bit of that, isn't there, for the ladies. And as we're knocking back a quick supper I nearly ask him, what do you think about this Wolfenden report thing? Not cos I'm… not because I'm worried. Just… interest, you know. But I don't say anything. We go to the pictures and he holds my hand. As we're walking home, about halfway, without stopping or looking at me or anything, he says out of the blue: 'I'd miss you, Alice.'

She smiles.

Fade to black.

i miss the war

matthew baldwin

First performed by **Ian Gelder**
on screen, as part of the BBC Studios production *Queers*
on BBC Four,
and on stage at The Old Vic, London, on 28 July 2017.

1967.

JACK – *sixties, smartly dressed – sits at a table with a glass of dry sherry. Sometimes he is playing to the gallery, sometimes not. His camp is for effect.*

I love sherry, because it's just a little bit too strong. I like a small glass first thing, just so I can feel my heart in my chest. Sip sip sip. Like an old dowager – which suits me now I'm respectable. But we'll come back to that.

He sings the last three lines of the third verse of 'Dedicated Follower of Fashion' by The Kinks.

Oh, I love this one. It's bona. (*Loudly to the room.*) Fantabuloza!

He nods to someone close by.

Oh yes, dear. Yes please and thank you, dry sherry.

None of your Harvey's Bristol! Look at all these bright young things. Enough to make your head spin. They're beautiful. Like kittens in a shop window, gambolling and pushing each other about. Oh, I could eat them all. I might at that.

Me, with my handsome face all lined and my hair all grey. I call it distinguished. I could teach them a thing or two. If I had a whistle, I'd be like him in that film, Captain von Trapp, bossing around the little virgin from the convent – the polone with the butch riah who does twirls on the hills. Some of them like that, being ordered about. But they all come into my shop. They like to flirt a little and hear me talk the polari to them. 'Ooh! Vada that great butch lucoddy!' Makes them roar. It's in Duke Street, my place. Well, it's cheaper than Savile Row. I am the Duchess of Duke Street! Put all my 'ill-gottens' into my little tailoring establishment so I can now spend my dotage politely touching up young men with the heating on full blast. Bona. And then I come here every day after I've shut up shop. Might be some sport to be had.

There's a crackle in the air this week. Excitement. The burden of lilley law has been lifted from the homosexual. We may now practise our sexual offences without fear of prosecution. Well, provided it's behind closed doors, you keep your jacket on and don't frighten the horses. One of them comes trolling into my premises with the good news, bold as brass, but not actual brass. A beautiful chicken, slathered in cologne. His trousers are very tight, so that you can see his… front room. I made 'em like that on purpose. And well appointed it is too! His jacket is kingfisher blue.

He's got on a polo-neck sweater, cashmere. Bona! You'd have sworn he had got bored of playing a harp on a cloud and just bounced down into the West End for a lark. And his face – his eek! The countenance: divine! My arse was snapping like a Venus flytrap.

He's a chorus boy at the Drury Lane, spends the interval flashing his bum at the dressing-room window of the Fortune. Says there's another chicken on the other side smiles at him.

It's like semaphore for buggers, I suppose. Oh, this way, dear, this way! 'So what are you going to do now?' he asks me. Well, you know, now that it's all legal. Like he's done all the heavy lifting himself. 'Oh, think how it will change your life, Jackie! What will you do now?' 'Well, I'll do what I've always done. I'll, I'll praise God, I will laud and sanctify his name. I will lift up my voice to the heavens in constant jubilation. Allelujah allelujah, hosanna in the highest.' 'Oh, you're so funny, Jack,' he says. 'Well, I'm not trying to be funny,' I say, 'it is what I'm going to do. You just don't understand. Anyway now you're here, anything I can do for you, doll? How about a whisky? Is it too early for a couple of fingers? Oh, you bought a hat, didn't you? Well, if you're here to get your beaver-felt, I'm afraid it's not quite ready.' And he bounces off. And that's my lot. Like I say, apparently I'm respectable now. It wasn't always thus.

Fade.

I took the King's shilling in 1932. I don't want to be indiscreet,
heaven forbid, so I won't say which regiment. But it's the oldest
regiment in Her Majesty's Armed Forces, has a dolly red tunic
and a bearskin hat. I joined up at a good time. Well, they knew
better than to put me near a fight and the top brass always loved
me for my ability to polish them up and turn them out looking
like Cleopatra in her barge. Corporal Jack Edwards, best boot-
polisher around. In the early days of my career I did what I was
told and looked very smart. But one summer's evening, as I was
taking the air in St James's Park, I was pleased, nay delighted,
to discover that the meagre income provided by the King could
be easily supplemented by the generosity of older gentlemen.

He crosses himself.

Forgive me, Father, for I have sinned. I have been a rentboy, a
renter or as I prefer to say it, a 'rentleman'. I have supped from
the forbidden cup, I have whispered the love that dare not speak
its name – and I could tell you the price of a wank every year
since the abdication. This generation here, drunk on possibility
and privilege, will never know the happiness I did at that time. I
knew exactly where I stood. Usually that was in a cottage
cubicle tossing off a judge or a man of the cloth. I always loved
a clergyman customer! Well, it was my privilege to step out
with several 'princes of the church'. We all used to love them.
They'd cum quickly and they'd always pay what they said they
would. Well, that's a very Christian act in my book. Five
minutes tops. I'd be a few bob richer and there'd be spunk all
over my bearskin. I'm only joking, I wouldn't wear a busby to
suck a vicar's cock. I'm not a monster!

I spent the whole war in England, never set foot in a foreign
field. By the time it all kicked off, I was safely ensconced as
batman to a colonel, thank God. Well, that's a bona job. I
followed him around making sure he looked the part. London
may have been burning, but at least we'd look dolly while we
did it. Don't think me flippant if I say there are things I miss.
What I really loved was the darkness. The blackouts. We're like
eels, you see, my kind. Eels live at the bottom of the lake where
it's coldest and pitch black. They slither around and they

burrow in the mud. Sometimes they bump into each other, down there, in the mud. And it feels nice. They rub their cold, slippery eel skin against each other and they love it. But then they move on, slither on. And back then, I could find my way in the dark, you see. These oggles of mine were already accustomed to it. And everyone was moving around, all the time, constant motion. All in need of comfort really, all of them scared. Desperate for some kindness.

And then, best of all were… *Americans*. The Americans saved our bacon. Well, we'd have lost otherwise and I'd be speaking German, at best. Now, I've heard many a sermon from many a pulpit and they're always very keen to tell you about heaven. Heaven this and heaven that. Heaven shall be our reward for living a good life, by which they mean paying your taxes and not causing any trouble. Well, I can tell you, categorically, they're all wrong. Paradise, if it's to be found anywhere at all, is right here on earth. For I have seen the face of God, right here in the West End.

Just around the corner from here is a great big square and in the middle of it there's a statue of a sea captain and around him four bronze lions. And that day, standing by one of the lions is an American private with green eyes and curly hair. Blessèd is he that comes in the name of the Lord. And the sun is on his face. Hosanna in the highest. He's looking at me. A daytime look, full of cigarettes and advice. I can't tell the steam from his breath from the smoke of his cigarette. And he has no gloves. And he's looking at me. Not sizing me up to see what he can get.

And he has little apples in his cheeks. Little apples at his cheeks. And finally I understand why the Trojans fought their war, and why Orpheus looked back, and why the fucking nightingale was singing in Berkeley Square. He's looking at me. He doesn't even know what it means. I approach him for a light. He tells me his name, but I won't tell it to you. I suggest we take a turn around the square. We walked around London all that day. I bought him some gloves. He taught me some words in American and pestered me for fags. The war had been cruel to him. Most people had been cruel to him. But I gave him sips of whisky, to see the apples glow.

As the light started to fade, the fear set in. The dragons come at night, don't they? The terrible wail of the sirens and the scrambling haste to safe places underground. Those with an investment in the future want to clasp their precious progeny to their bosom and hunker down, exhorting God to grant them another dawn. But not me. I was in the presence of my God.

And for once it was the others that were subterranean and the likes of us roamed the plains. And for one night we were free. We kissed on the mouth in the street. We went to my room and I undressed him, cross-eyed with excitement and, for that night, we were abandoned to each other. I laid him out and worshipped every inch of his beautiful body by turn. I was lost in his arms. But it was easily worth the risk of staying aloft in an air raid. Had that been my last night on earth, then a lucky man was I. The next day he was gone. Slithered on...

Fade.

Two things you must always do before sex at my age. Cover all the mirrors and put on the wireless or whatever you want, just not silence. But definitely cover the mirrors. I once caught a glimpse of myself 'going at it'. It looked like one of those lions in East Africa eating a gazelle. Rubbing his nose in the viscera. I've seen it on *Zoo Quest*. If you care to ogle me for a moment you will see that I am a lesson in the art of growing old with dignity and elegance. I have, like the stately homes of England, been somewhat in decline since the end of the war. My paintwork is peeling, my plumbing is Victorian and my servant's entrance is badly in need of attention. I know what I am and what I like. I make the most of what I've got. I play the hand I'm dealt as best I can. I come here every day and more often than not I do well. I'm generous to renters, pay them what I say I will.

Maybe even the rentlemen will dry up now. Have their heads turned by the possibility of living together like Mum and Dad in their little houses. Is that really what they want? Sex is more fun if you do a little bit of groundwork. Well, Christ, I've raised it to an art form! It's a kind of hunting. You send out signals, a bit of polari here and there, see what's on the radar. It's a thieves' cant, for heaven's sake. It's supposed to protect you from lilley law. It's not supposed to be on the wireless every day for the amusement of bored palones. I'd say 'Bona to varder your dolly old eek, dear! Come on, doll, let's go for a bevvy somewhere ajax so I can ogle the dish on that omi.' Understand? No? *Good*.

Trust me, homosexuals will be no better off than they are now, or my name's not Cassandra. And my name's not Cassandra. We will be forced to swallow the great lie that romance happens only once and that love is for ever. That's just not true. Why do you think normal people are so unhappy? Because they have unrealistic expectations. I am what everybody learns to fear. The lowest of the low. A dangerous, predatory homosexual, the kind that lurks silently, waiting to corrupt the healthy manhood of this septic isle. That's exactly what I am and they can all fuck off. I'll be in my tailor's shop. They're walking straight into a trap. But not me, dear. No point in that. Nanty point. They won't catch me.

It's a short walk from Duke Street to Trafalgar Square. I walk there every day. I stand in the same spot. I look over to the lion. I make my devotions. I remember the apples. A shorter walk still from the square to this place. A watering hole where the gazelles gather and the hunting is good. I've been doing it all my life and I'll do it in my lean and slippered pantaloons, I hope, because you never know what's coming round the corner. I want to fall into someone's arms, not someone's hands. I want to make my devotions to a teenage god with perfect skin, hot with life and blushing.

He touches his face.

'What secret shame doth rose thy Ganymede cheek?' I know.

He sings the opening lines to 'Dedicated Follower of Fashion'.

He slithers on.

Fade to black.

more anger

brian fillis

First performed by **Russell Tovey**
on screen, as part of the BBC Studios production *Queers*
on BBC Four,
and on stage at The Old Vic, London, on 31 July 2017.

1987.

PHIL, *twenty-nine. White T-shirt, 501 jeans rolled up at the ankles, Doc Martens. Beanie hat with a blond tuft of hair poking out at the front. An eighties gay. Phil isn't camp, but he's not 'laddish' either. He's witty. Razor-sharp – most of the time. Bit catlike.*

I'm getting quite good at dying.

He picks up a folded script and gestures with it.

Mostly that's me in a bed, in a hospital, looking pasty and terrified. And tetchy. They expect you to be *tetchy*. Like, I had PCP for a single on Channel 4. Pneumocytis Pneumonia. Horrible job. Take after fucking take. The director comes to me, Dan his name is. He said, 'We need to see more... anger, yeah?' I said, '...Why?' He just looks at me, like it's obvious. 'Because the Government are doing nothing, yeah, there's no funding, and these fucking iceberg films they have on telly now, it's fucking criminal.' I said, 'I thought my character would probably be past anger by this stage. I'd probably be thinking much more practical things like is this going to hurt? Or will it be over quick? What would I have done with my life if I'd lived? Maybe. Could I have done things differently, been more careful, made different choices?'

Anyway he wanted anger, so he got anger. I channelled the anger I was feeling towards him and that helped. This is a key skill. Some actors can't draw on themselves, their experiences. I can. Though obviously I'm not dead yet so I've been having to make that up.

Then after that I did a film where I get stabbed by a serial killer who's picking on gays for some unknown reason, but obviously that was just a metaphor. When the police finally catch him even he doesn't know why he does it. I saw that when it went out, at the Curzon, and I could hear quite a few people sobbing in the audience when I pegged it.

I got a bit tearful myself, actually. See, it's the face. I look young and innocent. So you're immediately thinking, 'What a waste.' That's why I get the parts, I reckon.

The scene I'm really good at is the deathbed scene where the boyfriend shows up. More often than not I'm doing well health-wise when the complications hit so the sudden deterioration's a surprise, for both of us. He's sometimes older. Not always. Cute, obviously, but there is an awkwardness between us. It's not actually said, but you get the vague sense that he's been messing about in saunas and toilets and not taking precautions while I, of course, have been faithful as a puppy. So then there's the injustice of it too. I have a bit of a barney with him but I'm generally forgiving. I just go a bit *arch*, you know. Got my sparky sense of humour right to the end.

I had lunch with my agent and she's dead pleased I'm working and so am I, but it's getting a bit samey. I don't feel like I'm moving forward, you know. She reckons I should be grateful. 'You're really grabbing at their heartstrings, Phil, really making an impact.' I just worry they're gonna get sick of the sight of me. 'Him again. Dying. Again.' She wasn't having it. 'Characters you get are pivotal, Phil, pivotal. Everything around you changes once you're...' Gone. Yeah. I said it's awfully nice that my friends get really, really upset when I'm dead, and then kind of reassess their priorities and stuff. I just wish I made it past page eighteen. She said, 'You get the full fee.' I said, 'That's not the point.'

Still, it's work. She said there might be a role playing a bat thing on *Doctor Who*. 'Do they still make *Doctor Who*?' I said. 'Apparently, yeah.' Plus a bit part in an indie film. English mourner at funeral in New York. 'Can you do grieving?' I said, '...Probably.'

Truth is, I don't have much to draw on, there. I've been lucky. I know what it looks like, though. I've seen it, seen it often enough, too often. Horrible. Then out of the blue she asks me if

I get tested. I said it's none of her business. I don't, as it happens. I couldn't face it. I'd sooner not know, I'm just not strong enough. It is possible to *not* get it if you're careful. And by 'careful' I don't mean bloody celibate or monogamous.

I fucking love sex, me – bum sex mainly. But there is an underrated beauty to blowing a total stranger in a toilet cubicle that's hard to convey. And if you try to convey it it gets boring or icky quite quickly, so… no squatting on your haunches, knees must hit the floor, and eye contact throughout.

He finds himself getting horny and picks up the script.

Tcch. I could be blowing someone now if it weren't for this bloody 'death scene'. Agent's promised she'll get me a role that doesn't involve losing half a stone and whiting the face up, so – fingers crossed…

Fade.

Some weeks later.

I quite like doing 'coming out' scenes, though even there death crops up pretty quickly. I did a play where I was Liverpudlian. So it was dead bitter but really funny – like corrosively funny. The mother's mopping the floor and I drop the bombshell. We have a row, I throw in, 'What d'you want me to do, get married and be unhappy?' She comes back with, 'Why not, that's what I bloody did.' Mother gets the best lines. The gay boy is the feed. Then of course she realises I'm not done with the bombshells and the full horror of her situation dawns on her. Her little Billy: gay *and* dead, in quick succession. 'More than a poor girl's heart can take.'

The upshot is she loses her faith. That was at the Finborough, so while she's rowing with the bishop at the funeral I slip out early and get down The Coleherne. There's a bloke goes there some nights, Simon. Fucking… whoo, the legs. Dancer's legs. And sorry, I actually *am* a size queen, I make no apologies. Simon… fits the bill. The best fuck ever. I've kind of got a top Top Ten in my head and for a long time it was a guy I met in Portsmouth at

Number One, but Simon has knocked him off the top top spot. Dead fit. Proper man. Nice enough bloke as well, sense of humour. I don't normally talk to blokes down The Coleherne cos it risks breaking the spell, but, hasn't broken Simon's spell.

He claps his hands.

Agent called yesterday... got me an audition for a TV. New soap... gay character called 'Clive'... who *isn't* ill and, according to the man at the Beeb, *never* gets it – it's actually in the contract... just... *has a life*, has the same kind of plot lines as the other characters but 'from a gay perspective'... so that'd be progress. If I got it. He's also not camp, which is fairly important. Not that I can't do camp, but the days of Mr Humphreys are over.

Lads at school used to take the piss when that programme was on. Not of me. I'm not naturally camp, but I can go quite blokey, in fact. I should get put up for more straight roles really. I did play 'Angry Shopper' in *Albion Market*, but it wasn't established whether he was gay or straight, so... doesn't count. Nor does the bat thing on *Doctor Who*, not really. No, Clive isn't camp but he's not blokey, either. He's... (*As if quoting.*) sensitive, takes life seriously and may appear guarded when we first meet him. But underneath he's warm, emotional and soon becomes a popular member of the local community. I can play Clive standing on me head.

Fade.

His hair is combed down so he looks a bit older. He's reading a script, learning lines. He mutters a line several times, trying new inflections, each time getting a bit angrier.

'Oh, so now it's my fault, is it.'

'Oh so now it's my fault is it?'

'Oh – so now it's my fault is it?'

Clive is the most boring man ever presented on a TV screen, seriously.

Fretful fucking creep. Not camp, no: no sense of humour *whatsoever*. I've got this beige boyfriend like Clive Mark Two, only taller with a pierced ear. And the fucking hugging we get up to, oh scandalous. I can't get ill, obviously – of anything. The fucker isn't even allowed to cough. Plot line at the moment where I turn out to be fiddling my tax returns. So me and the boyfriend can 'build a beige life together'. I had thought fiddling the tax might lead to a prison story, which could be quite... meaty, but no. Clive's not fiddling *that* much. Of course he fucking isn't. Ugh!

Simon's not beige. That's one colour that Simon really isn't. So fit. We've kind of been seeing a bit more of each other. His suggestion. Threw me at first. We'd just got it on in The Coleherne – cubicle nearest the window...

He gets nasty, does Simon. Full palm-of-the-hand stuff. And we were having a pint in the front after, and he suddenly says, 'We could go and see a *film* or something.' The thought of us hand in hand buying popcorn... But we gave it a whirl, and... it was nice. He's strong, only a few years older than me, but he's lived – proper man. Like a big brother. Taps into something, you know? It's nice. His legs are incredible. I know he's more than just a pair of legs, but all the same.

I could actually play 'in love' these days – if the right part would only fucking come up.

He picks up the script, reads the line again, trying to give it some meaning.

'Oh so now it's my fault is it.' There's a line in next week's episode where the beige boyfriend says he's thinking of moving back to Hemel Hempstead. I have a feeling Clive's gonna go with him so that'll be the end of that. Yeah, good riddance to him.

I went back to the agent. She says Clive isn't 'easy to love'. 'And if you *are* dropped from the show, darling, at least you're not leaving in a wooden box.' Which is true. I just thought that I was... getting somewhere.

Still, I'm up for tour of *Bent* at the end of the month, so it's not all doom and gloom.

Fade.

Another night. PHIL *is upset and very defensive*.

I just think if you're entering into a relationship with someone you should be honest from the start – not hide any bombshells, pull the rug from under a bloke's feet. I was completely not expecting it, just sitting with him on the sofa watching a film and he comes out with it, 'By the way I'm positive.' He must've seen panic in me eyes because he immediately says, 'We've been safe. You're not in any danger.' Which calmed me down a bit. Still, I was shocked. He said it was more than just HIV, he actually had AIDS. 'But I'm okay. I'm looking after myself. I get regular check-ups, do all the right things. Yeah, I get scared sometimes, but I stand a good chance. I wanted to tell you because… well, it's important if were gonna… get more serious, then…' I didn't say anything, just nodded. Well, it's a lot to take in, isn't it?

We tried to just spend the evening together but an hour in he says, 'This silence isn't just you getting your head round the news, is it?' I just looked at him. After that he went off into the kitchen, and… I heard him crying… sobbing like a baby.

So that was that. Spell broken. Well and truly.

It'd be nice if I had some work to take my mind off him, but… see the fallow periods are part of the job. Trick is not to see one rejection as part of a trend. Time passes though, dunnit. I won't be in the 'Young and Innocent' market for ever. And then dying's not as in demand as it was. Which is ironic cos there's more dying now than ever, way more. But the circus has moved on. The doctors say it's heading towards a peak and with all the drugs coming up more people are gonna live longer and longer, be like normal lives. Well, that may well be true, but I wonder where it all leaves me.

I mean, the only thing to do once the eighties are gone will be to wipe the slate, press reset, start having 'fun' again. And then no one's gonna want to watch the stuff I made once it really is over. I mean, why would they look back on all that death. It's just depressing. It's no way to move forward, is it? So no repeat fees. My oeuvre will moulder in the archives.

I ran into him last week, Simon, in Tower Records. He doesn't go down The Coleherne now. He was there with his little BF. Smiley, cute enough, and clearly lady helium heels. Well, he'd have to be. We talked a bit but it was… a bit awkward. I came away wondering whether he'd even told the little boyfriend. It's none of my business.

I know what my future'll be. I'll get work: 'Quiet Single Bloke at Party'. Some swish loft apartment. Music. I'll be just right for the man who can't quite get into the swing of things. Some young blond lad'll come over and start on me: 'Oh smile, it might never happen…' And that'll be my cue… to wag my finger, to lecture, tell them what went on. What 'we' went through. They'll all listen, but it'll be uncomfortable. They'll all kind of exchange glances, let me say me piece and then I'll probably storm off. The blond lad'll say something funny to lighten the mood. Time was, it was me who had the funny lines. Sparky sense of humour, only back then I was dying and they're not.

He shakes his head with tears close.

What was I supposed to do? He broke the spell.

If finger-wagging really is all I have to look forward to then I'll have a lot to work with. Have you heard – the Department of Health's pulled its finger out? They're gonna print some information about AIDS in the papers. Only Thatcher's said no. They should just stick some posters up on lavatory walls and leave it at that cos normal people can't catch it, you see, and no one wants to read about arse fucking in *The Sun*, do they. *The Sun*: 'When you mess with nature, you've got it coming to you, mate' – *The Sun*. And we've got *Private Eye* telling us gay stands for 'Got AIDS yet?' That's a good one, innit.

He gets increasingly upset.

The Met Police raided The Vauxhall Tavern last week. The coppers were wearing rubber gloves to protect them from the *gay plague*. Stuff like that is happening to us. While hundreds of people are dying, our friends and our lovers, stuff like that is fucking commonplace. And it feels like the world's gone cold and mad. And I'll bet you, years from now if you want to go anywhere near this stuff on stage you'll have to do it tangentially, use some clever trick to keep things light because hey, being gay in the eighties was about more than just AIDS, wasn't it?

Was that angry enough?

Fade to black.

a grand day out

michael dennis

First performed by **Fionn Whitehead**
on screen, as part of the BBC Studios production *Queers*
on BBC Four,
and on stage at The Old Vic, London, on 31 July 2017.

1994.

ANDREW – *seventeen, young, hasn't quite found his 'look' yet, long overcoat – sits on his own. A glass of Coke in front of him.*

There's a vegetarian restaurant round the corner. Just round – a couple of streets from here. Completely veggie. I had a – falafel. It was nice. It was… Okay. Did you see the news, on telly, last night? No, just wondered. There's some bits in the papers. I checked in in WHSmiths. Tiny, you know. But that's not what I'm… You didn't see *News at Ten*, or…? No. Shit. Oh well!

He glances to another part of the pub.

Two fellas over there…

He smiles. Then, a different tack –

Can you believe they voted no? Can you believe it? I couldn't believe it! No, not 'no', I know. But – eighteen! It's almost worse than if they'd kept it twenty-one. There'd be some – honesty in that. 'We hate you and, you know… piss off.' At least that would have been consistent. But… 'Yeah, we'll make you slightly more equal.' Big wow. Of course it's better, I know that. Of course it is. But… it's 1994! Jesus. That's what – this fella said last night. That it was good that things were changing. But… it just makes you… I don't want to be tolerated, you know?

Got a… bit – falafel in me teeth.

It's impressive when you see it – the House of Commons. Have you been? It's bigger than it looks on telly. I'd just come down, on me own. Wasn't planning to. I hadn't thought of it, really. I knew the vote was coming up, the – reading of the bill. I've been following it. But then it was on the front page, that morning, that Derek Jarman had died and – um… You know. Not like it was a sign or anything. I don't believe in all that. But – I just thought, sod it, I should go. Show them that – we count.

You know, we do exist. It does matter, the things they're talking about. So…

I'm not a big fan or anything. I just know he's important – Jarman. I've seen his version of *The Tempest*. That was the first thing I saw at the art-house cinema back home. Never even knew they were a thing. And I taped *Blue* off Channel 4 a couple of months back. Haven't watched it yet. That's been the best thing about sixth form – discovering things like that. No one at my old school would've ever gone to something like that. Morons! There was this lad in my year – Darren Hardcastle – 'Daz!' – and all he'd talk about was wanking. He was obsessed! It's all he went on about. And if he wasn't banging on about wanking, he was punching people. You know, wanking or punching. I used to think, 'This is what prison must be like.' This is like – 1984! Couldn't wait to leave. I ran from that place. Metaphorically. Well, literally, if they'd arranged a scrap with the comp across the field. Hated it.

We were outside for hours, last night. Shifting round, trying to keep warm. Most people were in groups, actually. I don't know if they were friends or… um, you know, Stonewall, that type of thing. There were some banners and signs and people had candles. I mean, you needed candles cos of how bloody cold it was! I'm telling you! Flippin' 'eck! And it was a weird mix of excitement – cos of what it was – and… boredom, cos it took ages.

This lad looked at me a few times while I was there. I saw him looking. Caught his eye. He was… (huh!)… He was lovely.

I can be a bit shy.

Then finally someone came out to say it had been done, whatever time it was, late, and – came out of the House of Commons. I couldn't see who they were – and then you heard everyone starting to boo and you think, 'Aww…!' – cos we'd been out there for so long and cos, well, I don't know how many people there were, but – enough. You know, two hundred? Enough to feel like – cos I'm used to being on my own. You know? I don't know anyone else who's – gay. And last night, there's loads of us. And we're nice! You know, I was looking round and I was thinking, 'These are nice people.' So then you start to think, 'Well, of course they'll vote the right way. Why wouldn't they? What would be the point in not?' You start getting carried away with reason. And, I know… You shouldn't do that.

So this bloke comes out and he must have said they'd voted eighteen and everyone started to boo cos… I think we'd all convinced ourselves it was going to be sixteen, you know, it was going to be equal. So it was like a – kick in the teeth. And then we all sort of surged towards the Commons, towards the doors he'd come out of. It just happened. And police were there, a couple on horses, that kind of thing. And people are chanting and shouting and just sort of… pissed off, you know. And there's a bit of a scuffle and I did think, you know, just for a moment – is this…? Cos a policeman's helmet landed at my feet. But, it was nothing really. And then someone shouted, 'Let's go to Downing Street,' and so we all marched up there and there was some shouting outside the gates for a bit. And then we went up to Trafalgar Square and a group of people started sitting in the road, to block the traffic. And you go along with it, but I did feel a bit… um. Self-conscious, I suppose. But, also, like…

He sticks up two fingers.

You know, cos I was pissed off too. And the police were getting a bit – not mardy, but… It was late. And I think we could all tell it had run out of steam. But we were angry. That's the point. And what do you do? So, we did – that. For, you know. Ten minutes. Then everyone went home.

Fade.

And then you read this morning that there were scuffles between police and 'a minority out to cause trouble'. There was no 'minority out to cause trouble'. It was so… piddly! There was a bit of shoving and a bit of shouting, that's all. To read the papers, the bit there is, you'd think it was a small riot. That's kind of interesting, the distortion. I've never been part of something that's been reported before. We were just – fed up.

So I'd missed my train by this point. And this fella – Marcus – I'd been sitting in the road with, said do I want to come back to his. And I thought, 'Well…' But what do you do? I had nowhere to go. So I did. That's his name, Marcus. Well, course it is! Sorry.

He affects a Spanish accent.

Mark-oos!

We went back to his, his flat, and it was – I mean, it was fine. It was a bit… not… It was okay. I think I'd thought… I mean, it's stupid, I know it is, but I think I'd thought… people in London. But London's just a place, isn't it, like any other. But I suppose you think – 'London!'

I don't mean to sound snobby. It's not snobby. I'm not a snob. My mate Sean's proper bourgeois – though he'd have you believe he's working class cos his dad – I don't know, once drained a radiator or something. But I remember his face when I said we had our tea on our laps on a Sunday watching *Bullseye*. So, I'm not… you know, posh. Anyway. Err. He was asking what I did – Marcus – and I told him, said I was a student and he said he worked for the BBC, in Accounts. So that's interesting, isn't it? Kind of. And I'd said, at the start, that I just needed a place to stay until I could get a train home in the morning, and he'd said that was okay. I was giving off the right vibes, I think. So, it was cool. He's a lot older than me. He's thirty, but he was, um – you know. Nice. He made us some toast and, um, put the heat on. So… it was fine. He had this jam that's made without any sugar. And we talked a bit. He said he'd been on a few, uh, marches and things, you know. Not just – gay. Other stuff. Poll tax and… So that was interesting. And we talked about last night. Called them bastards! Put the – what is it? Put the world to rights. And then he said, 'At least it means *you're* legal now' – cos I'm eighteen. I mean, I'm actually seventeen, but I'd told him I was eighteen cos I thought seventeen sounded a bit young.

Stupid, isn't it? And, I think, when he said that, I thought, '*Right*'… you know? But I just kind of laughed it off. So then he said he should go to bed and he went to get some bedding for me, for the sofa. And…

I think he thought I was a virgin. Which I'm not. But, I mean…
I'm not *not* a virgin. But, when he came back in the living
room, with the bedding, he was starkers. And I thought –

He exhales – 'Blimey!'

But then I thought, 'Maybe that's just what he does.' Sean – my
mate – sleeps in the nude. Never occurred to me that was a
thing you could do until I stopped round his. Well. A lot hadn't
occurred to me until I stopped round his. Anyway, I was sitting
down on the sofa, and he dropped the duvet and pillows next to
me. The duvet didn't have a cover on. The things that go
through your head. I thought – Mum'd never give someone a
duvet without a cover on it. So then he was there –

He holds up his hand indicating something near his face.

You know. 'Hello, boys.' So I'm kind of…

*The expression of a polite person who has, next to their face, a
cock.*

And he put his hand out and stroked the back of my head. You
know, just softly. And that was actually quite nice.

Sounds pathetic, doesn't it? And I'm not an idiot. I knew
what… you know. Cards were on the table. But I thought, 'He's
letting me stay over. And he's not – he's quite nice… Looking, I
mean. He's all right. He's not Kristian Schmid, but…' So I… I
put him in my mouth. And that seemed to go down well. And
then – a minute or two later – he stood me up and – kissed me.
And I thought, right, I've got to decide now. You know? If I'm
not up for this, I've kind of got to say something now. Cos you
don't want to be rude. But I didn't say anything. And so he led
me through into his bedroom and he said to me, 'Is this all
right?' And genuinely, for a split-second, I thought he was
asking about the room and I did think, 'Well, now we know
what Athena does with its remaindered stock.' But he had my
top off by that point and…

I felt kind of separate from it. Like I was watching myself. You
know – like Brecht! *Verfremdungseffekt!* And I was kind of
talking to myself, saying, 'Is this all right? Is this okay?' You

know, keeping calm. In my head! Not… I think that might have put him off.

It was just nice to – not be rushed, you know? Cos, I suppose… everything I've done up to now has been… at parties, with… lads from college who… Well, you've got to take advantage of the moment, you know? I say lads. Makes it sound like there's hundreds. There's not, believe me! I just mean – well. I just mean Jamie Flynn, I suppose. And Sean.

We… Not regularly, you know, not – If he's drunk and… in the right mood… And… I kind of know how to – be in the right place at the right time. But, well, it's an art more than it is a science. And you've either got one eye on the door or – worse – you've got to kind of prep yourself in case he… loses the mood or – after – decides it didn't happen. I don't mean nasty. Just…

So. It was really the first time it felt… legitimate. Doing… anything. With an accountant! I didn't have a clue what I was doing, I'll be honest. But well, he didn't – you know. He was nice. Patient. He kept talking to me and checking I was okay. I almost wished he wouldn't. I almost wanted him to just – go for it. Almost.

And I think weirdly – and this feels weird, now I come to think about it – but because I didn't madly fancy him, it meant I could – relax a bit more. It didn't seem as… important as it might have done. I could just – do what he told me and weirdly, that was kind of easier… I think. I mean, it wasn't easy, really, but…

While we were doing it – I can't believe I'm telling you all this. I had a – real coffee earlier, I think it's kicking in! – there was a moment where I was thinking, 'Two hours ago I was outside Parliament, and they told me I wasn't allowed to do this!' And that made me laugh! And that turned him on cos he thought it meant I was getting into it. And I *was* getting into it! But not cos of, or not just cos of him. I was thinking of all the… tossers who'd opposed it, opposed *me*, and I was thinking, 'If you could fucking see me now – fucking!'

And it felt great – oh, it felt great!

I mean, who'd have predicted I'd spend my first time thinking about – Lady Olga Maitland and Sir Nicholas fucking Fairbairn?! I doubt anyone's ever thought about them while doing it before – including people they're doing it with! If they do ever do it, the desiccated... *twats*.

I mean, I wasn't dwelling on them. I'm not a pervert. But it did give it a – a frisson!

He takes a drink.

I've never said 'frisson' before. Only ever seen it written down. One of those words, you know, like – (*Mispronouncing as three syllables.*) hyperbole.

And then – after – he turned the light off and he held me while he fell asleep. And... all I could think was, 'I hope Mum and Dad weren't watching the news'. Cos at one point, when we surged towards the doors of the Commons, that's when I'd seen the cameras.

Fade.

They had these big lights on the top of them, the cameras, like spotlights – cos it was dark, obviously – and I'd been trying to stay behind this big bloke in front of me, so I wouldn't be seen, but he moved out of the way just at the same moment that one of them swung round and I know it got me full in the face. And if that's been on *News at Ten* – I'm dead.

That's why I wondered if you'd seen it. Well, I'll find out later today, when I get back. I mean, I was thinking about him as well. Marcus. I was thinking, 'He could get in trouble for this.' But then I thought, 'Who's gonna say anything?' And, I mean, who is? Who cares?

They're quite dry, aren't they? Falafels. My friend, Alissa, she's a vegetarian. I mean, not just a vegetarian, she is quite fussy as well. You know, fries everything in water. She's got this, um... futon. Tofu! Instead of chicken. Have you tried it? I had some once. I wouldn't go mad. It's not really a substitute.

He's got his hand on his leg now. Those two blokes. It's just nice to see. You know, Nottingham, there's nothing. Gatsby's. MGM on the first Monday of every month. But, here... it's not lunchtime yet!

My two hopes are: that there won't be much coverage – that's quite a good bet, that it won't be on at all or that they'll only show one or two seconds so I'll be really unlucky if I'm on it – or that Mum and Dad weren't watching last night.

He pulls a face – 'unlikely'.

Or that they *were* watching and I *was* on it but they didn't see me. Cos they won't be looking for me. They won't be expecting me to be there. They think I stayed round Sean's last night. I'm kind of looking forward to telling him about it. Sean. I think I'll feel a bit better around him now.

It *was* good fun.

Funny, isn't it? Cos if they'd said yes – if they'd made it sixteen... I'd have gone straight home.

Fade to black.

something borrowed

gareth mclean

First performed by **Alan Cumming**
on screen, as part of the BBC Studios production *Queers*
on BBC Four,
and by **Mark Bonnar**
on stage at The Old Vic, London, on 28 July 2017.

2016.

STEVE *walks into the empty pub dressed in a suit for a wedding. He stops and looks at the table with wedding cake and glasses.*

When I was wee and we'd be out in the car, and we'd pass a wedding at a church or outside a registry office, my mum would, without fail, slow down, roll down her window, and shout out, 'Don't do it, you mad fools!'

In retrospect, I think she was still processing her feelings about the divorce. But we just thought it was funny. Every time. Really funny. Though not if you were a reluctant bride, with acute hearing.

Such incidents bred in me a suspicion – a certain uncertainty towards marriage, towards men. Towards making promises amid pomp and circumstance. Towards institutions and The Done Thing. What one ought and what one not. Oh, my scepticism is a rich inheritance. The family fortune from my mother's side. But here I am.

He takes cue cards for his speech from his pocket.

Which is why I have to get this right. Which starts with getting *this* right. All those Jaffa Cakes, inhaled for inspiration, can't have died in vain.

He clears his throat, refers to the cue cards and starts his speech.

Once upon a time, a plucky young man went on an adventure miles from home. In a magical kingdom in a faraway land, he met a handsome prince who spent all his days bringing joy to the lives of others. One night, at a ball where all the beautiful people in the kingdom had gathered, the handsome prince spoke to the man, who was minding his own business while desperately trying to get served at a bar, where, yet again, he had forgotten to take off his cloak of invisibility.

So kind was the prince that he bought the plucky young man a drink. And so gracious was the man that he asked the prince to dance. And the dance was so entrancing that everyone else in the room vanished, the world stopped spinning, and it was just the man and the prince in each other's arms, on top of the world. With only Lady Gaga for company. Now there's a threesome.

Pause for applause. Wild applause. Possibly some cheering. Obviously, if I fill in a few details, the magic of the story may pale – as magic often does when you see its mechanics. The adventure was a fortnight in Florida. The ball was a club playing 'Bad Romance'. The plucky young man was young-ish. And the prince wasn't a prince at all, but another plucky young man on an adventure of his own. That his adventure was working on a roller coaster in a theme park gets bonus 'OMG points' in my mind, but then I've always loved roller coasters – real and emotional. Lest you hadn't noticed.

Of course, this story isn't like the fairytales I was raised on. No horse-drawn pumpkins. Way too many homosexuals. I do have a story about three bears but NSFAJ. 'Not Suitable For Aunty Janice.' Or anyone else, mind you. No, people like me didn't feature in the stories I was told growing up. It felt as if I didn't exist. Even if there were characters like me, they were hall-of-mirrors distortions that made me feel like if I didn't want to exist. I had a go at ending my existence back then. But I was as good at suicide as I was at physics, so I lived and learnt. It's painful to be invisible in other people's stories. But there is a sliver of liberation. You can tell your own story. You can author your own life. There is no script to stick to.

Which is fucking terrifying. And quite exciting. And fucking terrifying.

He holds up his cue cards.

Not that scripts can't be useful.

For me and my people. Oh my god, 'My People'? For me and other gay people, we now have the opportunity – the right – to have the fairytale wedding that others have always had. Even just for a day, we can be handsome princes and/or/and beautiful princesses – though inevitably some of us will end up more Princess Margaret than Kate Middleton.

We – the gays – can now tell, out loud and proud, our stories. And everyone – yes, even you Aunty Becky, who told me I was making my life difficult with my 'choice' to be gay – has a better life because of it. Me having the right to get married doesn't take anything away from anyone else. Rights aren't like cake: me having some doesn't mean you get less. And speaking of cake...

He breaks off from his 'script'.

Too worthy? Too wordy. Too twee. Too angry? Am I angry? Maybe I should start a fight, set fire to something. Uncle Frank, perhaps.

Bloody straights. Not only do they go around shoving their 'lifestyle' down everyone's throats but they've also exhausted every aspect of getting married, made every possible choice into a cliché. And only now, when it's on its last legs, do they wheel in the gays for a vital refresh. After all this time.

He looks at his watch.

Hardly any time at all. Not just a Big Day but Monumental. Part of me wants the formality and frivolity over and done with, so life can go back to 'normal'. Another part of me wants to live in perpetual anticipation, in the thrall of the imminent thrill. And another part of me wonders if it's a good idea at all.

Even in victory, you lose something. The feeling of being the rebel, the subversive, the outlaw. I know: never happy with what I've got. Until him.

I personally have no reservations, no nerves, no niggles, no last-minute jitters, no brief or lengthy reconsiders for the-love-before-this-one or for my first or for the-one-that-got-away. Or the-one-that-required-an-escape. Not even for my great-unrequited-who-might've – if I'd asked. No, the answer to the proverbial question when popped was never going to be 'No'. It's at moments like that you realise, despite your best efforts, you've still been indoctrinated with old-fashioned, romantic, sentimental ideas of what love is and how it plays out. I read it described once in a book as having 'fairytales stuck in your innards'. Love is a sentimental tapeworm.

Sometimes, I still can't believe I'm having a wedding. Getting married is one thing but a wedding? And a wedding of this size. A wedding we technically cannot afford. A wedding at which I'm already having an issue with the table decorations.

He lifts up a Christmas cracker.

From Aunty Sheila. She normally buys them half price in the January sales for the following Christmas. Only this year she decided my getting married was a 'special enough' occasion to get them out six months early. A 'special enough' occasion. And the fact that she's not sure she'll be around come Christmas, her bowels 'being what they are'. All I care about is they don't pull focus today – the bowels, not the crackers. These crackers won't – they're from Asda. But let's not get entangled in Sheila's innards.

Fade.

Marriage: an institution for the insane to which you commit yourself voluntarily. For those that won't commit or submit, those that can't, won't or don't fit, there are other institutions. Asylums and prisons, say. In the end, we all find our place – or are put in it. The kitchen, the bedroom, the attic, the cellar, the cemetery. I read *The Handmaid's Tale* at school. It was very illuminating. I loved school. Well, I loved learning. I could have done without the relentless bullying, having the shit kicked out of me on a weekly basis, and kids I didn't even know shouting across the playground at me: 'Die of AIDS, you fucking poofter!'

Children. So adorable. You can't really blame them. Little pitchers. What gets poured in, gets poured out. And what got poured in then was Section 28, Tory family values, the 'gay plague', and '*EastBenders*' on the front of *The Sun*. Because I was the danger – me. I never felt that, of course. I wish I'd felt dangerous. What I felt was anxious, fearful most of the time, forever poised for fight or flight. Needing to read every room in an instant, to assess the potential threats – who the alphas were, who to avoid and who to make an ally.

From that – the last one left standing unpicked at PE, the saddo sitting out the school-disco slow-dances because he couldn't wrap his arms round the one he wanted, the teenager looking for love in pissy public toilets and parks after dark – to this… Respectability. Propriety. Decorum.

He is fleetingly pained, thinking of what's lost and what's gained.

Perhaps everyone has their price. And maybe mine is measured in crockery and cookware on a John Lewis gift list. Or maybe it's measured in love and loving. From spoonfuls to right big buckets. And what I learnt about love, first and foremost, I learnt from Liza. Oh, my lovely mum, not Ms Minnelli. Although…

He feigns half-hearted jazz hands.

Terrific!

There was this one time, when I had got really badly beaten up by Grant Smiley at the swings and Mum went round to his house. Like a pocket tornado, she ripped strips off Grant's mum and scared the beejesus out of him. He steered well clear after that. Smiley's no so smiley then. Knights in shining armour come in all shapes and sizes. Mine was five foot nothing in her stocking soles.

I remember Mum having to decide whether to buy a pint of milk or a loaf of bread because we couldn't afford both. But I never remember having to choose between love and laughter. We had both, in abundance. Some shouting too, admittedly. Okay, a lot of shouting. Some screaming even, maybe, occasionally. But mostly, overwhelmingly… love.

When I told her that I'd met a man on holiday and he worked in
a theme park, she didn't bat an eyelid. When I brought him
home, she welcomed him with open arms and asked if, being an
American, he liked The Dixie Chicks. And then she said it was
'typical Steven' to win a man at a funfair when most people
make do with a goldfish.

He chuckles.

But she's always been the witty one in our family.

He reaches for the cue cards.

Which reminds me. There's going to be an Oscar Wilde quote.
Obviously. You can't have a gay wedding without an Oscar Wilde
quote. When I worked in a care home when I was at college, there
was an old blind man I read to sometimes. He loved Oscar Wilde.
Even said he's seen him once. And that's how I know this quote.

'All women become like their mothers. That is their tragedy. No
man does. That's his.'

That's not my tragedy. For better or for worse – mostly better –
I am totally turning into my mother. And I'm fine with that.
Though I suspect she'll always be the better line-dancer. I could
say, I suppose, that 'Today isn't about me, it's about her, about
seeing my lovely mum so happy.' And that wouldn't be entirely
a lie but, come on, let's face it – today is all about me. Me and
him. But mostly me. And him.

Him. The man who, when we first met, smelled of candy floss,
soap and everything-will-be-okay. Quite a heady combination.
My someone-to-dance-round-the-kitchen-with, my someone-to-
take-photographs-of. Someone-to-talk-to-all-day-and-spoon-
with-all-night. He loves my singing. Okay, he tolerates my
singing. And he even likes my cooking. He laughs at my jokes
and he lets me cry. He encourages me to be kind. He makes me
want to be a better man. And the best view ever isn't Uluru or
Iguazu, the Taj Mahal, the Grand Canyon or even Edinburgh as
seen from Arthur's Seat on a clear autumn day, with the Forth
shimmering in the distance. It's the nape of his neck when he's
lying asleep in my arms.

I know we don't get happily-ever-afters in real life. I'm a hopeless romantic, not a total fucking idiot. As my friend Russell said to me once, 'Even with the happiest couples, one of you dies first.' But first, there is such unalloyed joy.

We went to the supermarket yesterday and were wandering round, and at one point he took my hand, because that's the kind of thing he does. And instantly I got flustered. Residual anxiety. Remembrance of past battery. Enduring scars. Even though I know I'm hardly likely to get my head kicked in by the salad bar, PDAs can still make me nervous. And then he said, gentle as anything – and I'm not going to do the accent – 'If there's a gay kid in here with his folks, frightened that he's a freak, don't you think that it might give him hope seeing two guys wandering around, being themselves, getting their groceries like everyone else?'

If happiness is a place, it's the biscuit aisle in Sainsbury's – and anywhere else I am with him. And when we met, I'll never forget what he said when I introduced myself. 'Pleased to meet you, Steve. I'm Adam.' And then: 'And if that's the case, we should probably get married. Adam and Steve has a certain ring about it, don't you think?'

He holds up his hand to show he's wearing a ring.

Oh, and now it has got a certain ring about it. He liked it and he put a… Oh, don't spoil it, Steven.

He gets up on the stage, put the cards in his pocket and starts a speech without them.

This is the beginning of a new chapter in my story – our story. It continues tomorrow when we go back to where our tale began, and I get to meet Adam's extended Orlando family – which, funnily enough, does include a giant and a couple of dwarves. We may even stop off for a dance at the ball where the beautiful people are. Sadly they don't do glass slippers in my size – but then, when did I ever leave a club before midnight? Ladies and gentlemen, please raise your glasses to my… husband, the love of my life – Adam. To our always and forever, till death do us part, as hopefully-happy-ever-after as it gets.

He visibly relaxes, feeling he has said his piece.

I think it's better just off-the-cuff, from the heart. You can really overthink these things, can't you?

Fade to black.

**BBC Studios Pacific Quay Productions
in association with Can Do Productions,
The Old Vic, London, and BBC America**

Script Supervisors	SANDRA BRESLIN
	ANGELICA PRESSELLO
First Assistant Director	HELEN OSTLER
Second Assistant Director	PEBBLES HUGHES
Floor Runners	AARON McGAHON
	ELLIOT WENGLER
Art Director	FIONA COONEY
Production Buyer	REBECCA CHIDGEY
Construction	PRETTY SCENIC
Prop Master	DEAN HUMPHREY
Standby Props	PAUL MICHEL
Dressing Props	RON TOOTILL
Make-up Supervisor	CAROLINE GREENOUGH
Costume Supervisor	HELEN BOLTER
Focus Puller	NIALL CULLINANE
Clapper Loader	JOE MARTIN
Grip	EMMET CAHILL
Gaffer	PETER BRIMSON
Electricians	STEVE MURPHY
	JAMIE WHICKMAN
Boom Operator	ADAM MARGETTS
Titles	CHRISTOPHER LEWIS
Music	BRIGHT LIGHT
	BRIGHT LIGHT
Dubbing Mixer	SAMUEL CASTLETON
Colourist	ROSS BAKER
Online Editor	ADAM HALL
Sound Recordist	KIERON WOLFSON
Script Editor	SCOTT MEEK
Make-up Designer	KAREN HARTLEY-THOMAS
Costume Designer	CLAIRE FINLAY-THOMPSON

Production Designer	JO RIDDELL
Director of Photography	SUZIE LAVELLE
Editor	WILL OSWALD
Business Affairs Executive	ELAINE McINTYRE
Commissioning Editor	MARK BELL
Development Executives	DAVID DEVENNEY
	MIKE SMITH
Line Producer	ANNE McGARRITY
Executive Producer	PAULINE LAW
Producer and Director	MARK GATISS

The Old Vic

The One Voice monologue series was conceived by
Artistic Director Matthew Warchus

Directors	MARK GATISS
	JOE MURPHY
	MAX WEBSTER
Lighting Designer	MIRIAM SPENCER
Sound Designer	ANDREW SULLEY
Music	BRIGHT LIGHT
	BRIGHT LIGHT
Costume Designer	CLAIRE FINLAY-THOMPSON
Casting Director	JESSICA RONANE CDG
Production Manager	DOMINIC FRASER
Deputy Production Manager	ANTHONY NORRIS-WATSON
Production Stage Manager	SAM HUNTER
Stage Manager	IAN STEPHENSON
Head of Wardrobe	FIONA LEHMANN
Deputy Head of Wardrobe	LOUISE ASKINS
Head of Stage	JAMES BOSTON
Deputy Head of Stage	STEVE GRANT
Deputy Head of Electrics	EDEN THORNTON
Electrics Chargehand	ANDREW STUTTARD

One Voice is funded by the TS Eliot Estate

Author Biographies

Matthew Baldwin

Matthew Baldwin is a writer and actor living in North London. In 2013 Matthew and his colleague Thomas Hescott developed *The Act*, a play for one actor, for Ovalhouse. Matthew was nominated for an Off-West End Award for Best Actor and jointly with Tom in the category of Best New Playwright. In 2014 *The Act* transferred to Trafalgar Studios in the West End with Matthew reprising his role. Also in 2014 Matthew and Tom wrote *Outings* for James Seabright Productions, which enjoyed a successful run at the Gilded Balloon at the Edinburgh Festival Fringe and subsequently a national tour featuring Simon Callow, Julie Hesmondhalgh, Stephen K Amos and Jim Davidson, and a celebrity gala performance at the Lyric Theatre, Shaftesbury Avenue, in June 2017 with a cast including Tom Walker, Fisayo Akinade and Hardeep Singh Kohli. He is currently working on a new play, *Casa Marco*, about a gay brothel in contemporary West London. Notable theatre work as an actor includes Robert Russell in *46 Beacon* (Hope Theatre), The Better Argument in *The Clouds* by Aristophanes (Cambridge Arts Theatre), Justiniano in *Westward Ho* (White Bear), and *24 Hour Plays* (Old Vic New Voices). He alternately played the Dame and the Villain in four seasons of the multi-award-winning Above The Stag pantomimes. He has played an Ugly Sister and Abanazer in two seasons of panto at the Queen's Theatre, Barnstaple. Film and TV work includes Dan in *Love Bite* (Stone Circle Productions), *Material Girl* (BBC), and Augustus Pike in *The Dark Room* (Cinema Hades).

Jon Bradfield

Jon Bradfield is the co-writer and songwriter of London's longest-running and most popular alternative pantomime series, having created eight adult Christmas shows for Above The Stag Theatre including most recently *Beauty on the Piste* and

Tinderella – Cinders Slips It In, each of which played fifty sold-out performances. With the same co-writer, Martin Hooper, he wrote the play *A Hard Rain* which has been performed in London and New York and is also published by Nick Hern Books. He also wrote the music and lyrics and co-wrote the book for the musicals *Get 'Em Off* and *He Shoots! He Scores!* Jon has contributed to the long-running topical sketch show *News Revue* at the Canal Cafe Theatre. He has written articles for the *Guardian*, *Attitude* and *Exeunt*. Jon is also a theatre marketer and graphic designer.

Jackie Clune

Jackie Clune is a writer, actress and singer who lives in East London. She has published numerous features for the *Guardian* (*Weekend* magazine), *Daily Mail* (*Femail*), *Mail on Sunday* (*YOU* magazine), *Observer*, *Independent*, *Red* magazine, and *The Scotsman*. In 2012 she had her own column in *Top Sante* magazine. In 2004 she published her first novel *Man of the Month Club* (Quercus UK, Penguin USA), and in 2006 *Extreme Motherhood: The Triplet Diaries* (Macmillan, serialised in *Femail*). She has just written a monologue for BBC Two, and is currently writing a one-woman play. She is the mother of four children, including a set of naturally conceived triplets. She is a regular contributor to the Jeremy Vine show on BBC Radio 2, and has also contributed to various BBC Radio 4 arts programmes (*Front Row*, *Woman's Hour*, *Loose Ends*). She is currently writing her second novel for the young-adult market.

Michael Dennis

Michael Dennis is an experienced Company Stage Manager, who has worked for the Royal Court Theatre, Donmar Warehouse, National Theatre, Royal Shakespeare Company, Hampstead Theatre, National Theatre of Scotland, Old Vic and Regent's Park Open Air Theatre, amongst many others. His other plays include *Dark Sublime*.

Brian Fillis

Brian Fillis wrote the screenplay for *Against the Law*, a BBC
Two drama-documentary about the arrest and conviction of gay
journalist Peter Wildeblood. The drama opened the 2017 BFI
Flare Festival and stars Daniel Mays, Richard Gadd and Mark
Gatiss. Brian's previous TV work includes *The Curse of
Steptoe*, a single drama for BBC Four, which aired in March
2008 and won the RTS Award for Best Single Drama. His
television debut was his adaptation of his cult comic play *Fear
of Fanny* for BBC Four, starring Julia Davis and Mark Gatiss,
which was nominated for a string of awards including a
Broadcast Award for Best Single Drama and an RTS award for
Julia Davis. Brian was himself nominated for the Breakthrough
Talent Award by BAFTA in 2007. In February 2009, *An
Englishman in New York* had its world premiere at the Berlin
Film Festival, followed by a broadcast on ITV1. The drama told
the story of Quentin Crisp's latter years in New York and
starred John Hurt – thirty-four years after he first portrayed
Crisp on screen. In 2010, *Excluded*, a single drama for BBC
Two, was seen by 1.4 million viewers as part of the channel's
School Season, and in 2011 Brian created and wrote three
episodes of *Sirens*. He recently worked on episodes for Simon
Beaufoy's upcoming FX series *Trust*, and *Tatau*, a BBC Three
drama which aired in 2015. Brian has several projects in
development, including *Endangered*, a returning series with
Simon Maxwell at Channel 4, and a feature biopic provisionally
titled *I (Who Have Nothing)* with Rainy Day Films.

Mark Gatiss

Mark Gatiss is an actor, writer and producer. He first found
success with *The League of Gentlemen*, with whom he won the
Perrier Award at the Edinburgh Festival Fringe in 1997, and
went on to enjoy a radio series and three TV series on the BBC
and big-screen outing in 2005. He has written nine episodes of
Doctor Who since its return to television in 2005 and has
appeared in the show twice. He is perhaps best known as the co-
creator and co-writer of the award-winning global phenomenon
Sherlock in which he also plays Mycroft Holmes. Other notable
television credits include *London Spy*, *Wolf Hall*, *Coalition*,

Mapp and Lucia, *The Crimson Petal and the White*, *Nighty, Night*, *The Wind and the Willows* and *Sense and Sensibility*. Film credits include *The Knot*, *Denial*, *Absolutely Fabulous*, *Dad's Army*, *Our Kind of Traitor*, *Bright Young Things* and *Starter for Ten*. Theatre credits include *Coriolanus*, *The Recruiting Officer*, *The Vote* (Donmar Warehouse), *All About My Mother* (The Old Vic), *Season's Greetings* (National Theatre), *55 Days* (Hampstead), and *Three Days in the Country* (National Theatre), for which he won an Olivier Award for Best Supporting Actor.

Keith Jarrett

Keith Jarrett writes poetry and short fiction and is a former London and UK Poetry Slam Champion. He runs workshops, and has performed at and co-ordinated poetry festivals in English and Spanish. His poetry show *Identity Mix-Up* debuted to five-star reviews at the Edinburgh Festival Fringe in 2013. Subsequently, he completed the pioneering Spoken Word Educators programme, teaching in a secondary school while studying for an MA at Goldsmiths University. He also won the Rio International Poetry Slam Championship at the FLUPP Favela Literary Festival (Brazil, 2014) and was a Fiction Fellow at Lambda Writers' Retreat in Los Angeles (2015). Since being awarded a PhD studentship at Birkbeck University of London, Keith is now researching the culture of Caribbean Pentecostalism in London, while writing his novel. His latest book of poetry, *Selah*, was released in June 2017.

Gareth McLean

Gareth McLean trained as a journalist and has written for *The Scotsman*, *Guardian*, *Radio Times*, *Attitude* and *Buzzfeed*. He began working in television in 2013, as a storyliner on *Coronation Street*, where he worked for two-and-a-half years. During that time, he helped kill Hayley Cropper. After a stint on *Emmerdale* – where, unusually, he doesn't recall killing anyone – he started writing his own scripts and working in drama development for companies such as Playground Entertainment. *Something Borrowed* is his first script commission.

Switchboard
LGBT+ helpline

Switchboard is one of the UK's longest-running, volunteer-led charities serving the LGBT+ communities. As a national helpline, we serve on average 15,000 callers a year across phone, instant messaging and email. However you need to reach us, you can, from 10 a.m. to 10 p.m. every day.

Whilst we were established to provide vital signposting and information to LGBT+ communities, we are a service open to all. We talk to people from all across the UK, wishing to discuss issues ranging from sexuality, gender identity, mental and sexual health, isolation and more. Whether this is a personal challenge or one facing a friend or family member, we are a confidential, non-directive service – we don't tell people what to do and we don't judge. We're here to listen and support people to make informed decisions for themselves. Every call is unique, and Switchboard prides itself on responding to the changing needs of our communities by providing a service that's continually evolving and relevant.

We've been here since the first days of the AIDS crisis. And we're still here now.

The milestones of the LGBT+ communities can be traced in the calls we've taken. Our volunteers have responded to heartbreaking calls on loss and despair to triumphant messages of acceptance and love.

We don't know what issues the coming decades will bring, but we're determined to be here, answering people's calls, all the while.

Contact us, 10 a.m. to 10 p.m., 365 days a year

Phone   0300 330 0630
Email   chris@switchboard.lgbt
Instant messaging   www.switchboard.lgbt